AF661441

That society is the greatest, where the highest truths become practical. That is my opinion, and if society is not fit for the highest truths, make it so, and the sooner, the better. Stand up, men and women, in this spirit, dare to believe in the Truth, dare to practise the Truth!

Swami Vivekananda

No law or ordinance is mighter than understanding

Plato

Science can denature plutonium, but it cannot denature evil in the heart of man

Albert Einstein

I will give up twenty thousand such bodies to help one man. It is glorious to help even one man

Sri Ramakrishna Paramahansa

This life is short, the vanities of the world are transient, but they alone live who live for others, the rest are more dead than alive

Swami Vivekananda

Knowledge is the most democratic source of power

Alvin Toffler

The control of knowledge is the crux of tomorrow's world-wide struggle for power in every human institution

Alvin Toffler

Corporations determine far more than any other institution the air we breathe, the quality of water we drink, even where we live. Yet they are not accountable to anyone

Robert Monks and Nell Minow, 'Power & Accountability

Peoples are looking for business leaders to exercise true leadership. We expect more than high quality products and services from corporations. We are concerned about the environment. We worry about the gulf between the haves and have-nots. We want corporations to demonstrate higher values

Alvin

Black Truths

Corporate Character – the Invisible Compass

A K Mandal

Manas Publications
New Delhi - 110 002 (India)

MANAS PUBLICATIONS

(Publishers, Distributors, Importers & Exporters)

4402/5-A, Ansari Road

(Opp. HDFC Bank)

Darya Ganj, New Delhi-110 002 (INDIA)

Off. 23260783, 23265523, Res. 23842660

Fax: 011-23272766

E-mail: manaspublications@gmail.com

www.manaspublications.in

© A K Mandal

2016

ISBN 81-7049-272-6

Rs. 495/-

No part of this book can be reproduced, stored in a retrieval system, or transmitted in any form, by any means, including mechanical, electronic, photocopying, recording, or otherwise, without prior written permission of the publisher.

The views expressed in this book are those of the author and not necessarily of the publisher. The publisher is not responsible for the views of the author and authenticity of the data, in any way whatsoever.

Designed at

Manas Publications

Printed in India at

RK Print Services, Delhi

and published by Mrs Suman Lata for

Manas Publications, 4402/5-A, Ansari Road

(Opp. HDFC Bank),

Darya Ganj, New Delhi-110 002 (INDIA)

Dedication

I dedicate this book to the memory of my parents who had high expectations and dreams which I could not fulfill as they desired. I am grateful to them for teaching me the importance of honesty and ethics during my formative years. I always draw inspiration and courage from the values they have taught me in guiding my mind to face the reality of life.

This book is also dedicated to those known or unknown people who genuinely believe in social good and are working towards that direction in their sphere of activities.

Preface

Many management, marketing and economic theories were written and re-written, many books were published and re-published, many jargons or concepts were invented/ reinvented and propagated in the corporate marketplace–which in reality most of the people can't keep track of or remember and thus, these so-called theories or jargons have had limited relevance except occasionally stimulating intellectual debates, discussions, conflicting interpretations, disagreements and confusions. Some of the famous jargons, concepts or theories are listed below:

- TQM (Total Quality Management)
- Six Sigma
- Re-engineering
- Value Engineering
- Right Sizing
- Restructuring
- Turnaround
- CRM (Customer Relationship Management)
- CVM (Customer Value Management)
- CEM (Customer Experiential Management)
- ROI (Return On Investment)

- ROC (Return On Customer)
- CSR (Corporate Social Responsibility)
- Theory X,Y and Z
- EVA (Economic Value Added)
- ISO accredition
- Social marketing

Selling theories, jargons and expectations has become a big business. Re-invent an old theory or jargon, package it new and then advertise, promote, and sell. Conducting seminars on new jargons or theories, presenting articles, creating hype and expectations, has become a new fad. How many people really listen to those presentations? How many people really understand them?

This intellectual superficiality is continuing to take advantage of the fact of most people having limited attention due to chaos, confusion, job pressure and the desperation to protect their own careers. Everybody wants instant results or success. How many people really read those big books of socalled gurus? How many people really understand those jargons or theories? How many people really have the opportunity or the context, patience and sincerity to practice those theories except occasionally dropping those jargons to 'impress' others, or making a kind of PR exercise?

If we remove our intellectual hypocrisy, we will see the reality as being full of scandal, chaos, corporate misconduct, fraudulent activity, confusion, bankruptcy, cheating, social distrust towards business, and callousness of a section of corporate community who indulge in 'competitive extravagant lifestyle' when vast sections of our population does not have food, shelter and drinking water. It is time we start accepting the skeleton of corporate realities.

Unless we are sincere to accept the reality, no solution can be found and also it will be too late to take effective affirmative actions.

Many organisations have already started realising the futility of complicated models, strategies and planning. Theories having limited utility without fundamentals are in place. Many people started talking about 'capitalism with a human face', 'reform with a human face' or return on customer (ROC), CRM, CSR, social marketing etc etc. They have started accepting indirectly that fundamental to all theories is creation of the 'socio-economic value'.

Organisations are now realising the potential of social trust to improve their competitive context the quality of business environment in which they operate. Without creating socio-economic value, no organisation can become an 'institution'. In the 21st century only that institution will survive meaningfully in the long run since customers , civic community and society at large are evolving very fast. They are becoming more knowledgeable and aware of their rights. Also, they are becoming more and more demanding by each-day.

In the last thirty years, the incredible speed of change triggered by new technology and communication system–TV/internet–has literally transformed the consciousness of people across the globe. The radical social, political, economical, and other human-related changes that have taken peace in a such a short time span are historically unprecedented. Never has so much change occurred in such a short time, and never has so much knowledge and information became available to the public. Resultantly, there is a tremendous increase of awareness among people to bring change or a transformation of socio-economic environment.

The days of arbitrage or manipulation and control of information are over. Information is democratically and freely available. Customers have started understanding the power of information. They are aware of the socio-economic environmental issues. Technology and information have made possible alternative choices all this implies that we should sincerely start thinking to build 'institutions' instead of 'limited companies'. For survival, an organisation has to build social trust through genuine social innovations and investments.

Customers are part and parcel of the society and economy. How can you create new customers and satisfy them in a sustained manner without caring for the society? During the last hundred years, the world has created wealth at an exponential rate. However, distribution of wealth has become more uneven/skewed as the time passed. The disparities in income and wealth between the world's rich and poor are striking. The richest one percent of the world's population, approximately 60 million people, receive as much income as the poorest 57 per cent, 3.4 billion and 1.2 billion people– 20 per cent of world's population- exist on less than a dollar a day. As per one report, in 1999, the three richest people in the world were worth more than the combined GDP of the world's 34 poorest nations. Sustained growth of market for various goods and services will remain a pipe dream if the vast majority of people remain outside the income generation process.

Some facts as per FAO's report "*State of Food Insecurity in the World, 2004*": The number of undernourished people in the world rose by 18 million between 1995-97 and 2000-02, sharp reversal from the decline of 221 million in the population of the hungry in the previous five years. As per the report an estimated number of undernourished people in the world in 2000-02 was 852 million, of which 815 million were in the developing world, 28 million in the transition economies and 9 million in the industrialised countries.India alone had 221million hungry people, while China had another

142 million. The most shocking fact is that one child dies of hunger somewhere in the world every five seconds.Another is that each year about 20 million children are born underweight and that in countries like India and Bangladesh more than 30% of children are born underweight and it is, as Woody Allen rightly observed: 'Half the world is starving, the other half is on a diet'."

Some more startling facts as per the 10th Annual Unicef Report: More than one billion children half of the world's population of children suffer from poverty, violent conflict and the scourge of AIDS. Some 640 million children lack adequate shelter, 400 million have no access to safe drinking water; 270 million have no access to health care services and 140 million–mostly girls–have never been to school.

The World Day against Child Labour is observed every year by ILO. But what is the ground reality. As per ILO's own estimates there are one million children aged between 5 and 17 toiling in mines and quarries all over the world. As per ILO, majority of these mines and quarries are not mechanised and operate without adequate tools or safety measures. The work exposes children to risk of death and injury from tunnel collapses, accidental explosions, rock falls, exposure to toxic substances such as mercury and lead, and chronic health conditions such as silicosis, ILO experts point out. ILO Director General Juan Somavia said in a statement:" Children who work in mines and quarries are risking their health and safety and indeed their lives and action must be taken now." But the question is: who will take the action?

What is the relevance of top economists and management gurus or top educational institutes if 1.2 billion people are barely able to survive. Why should society respect these so-called intellectuals or corporate leaders?

In India, we have several big business houses, several business leaders, CEOs or Promoters–yet India's Human Development Index is 128th out of 174 countries. Isn't it shameful? We have crores of people who still do not have access to elementary education, healthcare, sanitation and drinking water. Isn't it shameful for us - the so called intellectuals/leaders? 26% of India's population is below poverty level and 44 percent population illiterate. India's literacy rate is 65% versus a global average of 80%. Thirtyfive million of our 192 million children between 6-14 years could not enroll and of those enrolled, another 15 million are habitual absentees. Drop out rates are staggering and only 31% complete basic schooling of grade ten.

The state of healthcare infrastructure in India is equally pathetic. The availability and quality of healthcare in the public health system has been deteriorating day by day. Nearly two-thirds of India's population lacks regular access to healthcare with inefficient and overburdened facilities, concentrated in urban centres, and acute levels of poverty with non-existent infrastructure in rural areas.Our bed-population ratio in 2004 is less than that of 205 of what it should have been as per WHO guidelines for the year 2004. Heathcare in private sector is unaffordable, especially for the poor, and is often irrational. As the NSSO data shows, between 1986 and 1995, the proportion of persons availing hospitalisation in the public sector dropped from 60% to 45%. At the same time, the average cost of hospitalisation increased by more than five times during the last ten years. Medical care has become so unaffordable that 40% of hospitalisation is paid for by taking loans or selling assets. An estimated two crore Indians are pushed below the poverty level every year due to inability to pay medical expenses. There is massive gap between the rich and poor in terms of access to healthcare, with a person from the poorest 20% of the population being six times less likely to be able to access standard medical care, compared to a person from the richest 20% of the population. 25% of the urban population have to sell assets or take loans to meet treatment expenses, while percentage is as high as 43% in rural areas.

Recent media reports on the poor quality of tap water in Indian metros undermine the validity of India as an emerging economic power, Water quality and availability may be only one of the parameters with which to measure a country's development rating, but it is a vital indicator of the quality of life. Water availability and sanitation are closely linked and which directly affect the health of the people. According to UN sources, worldwide, nearly one in every five people or 1.1 billion men, women and children have no access to clean water. The 2002 Earth Summit declaration stressed that making clean water available to all should be on top of every country's agenda. Availability of quality water is grossly inadequate in India. As per the latest NSS report, for 51 percent rural households, the major source of drinking water is tubewells; 27 percent depend on taps and 18 percent on wells. Almost 74 percent of urban population depend on taps for drinking water. Water-borne diseases are quite common in most parts of India. High arsenic concentration in underground water was found in most part of the country. Several water-borne diseases are caused due to water contamination by human waste; as per one estimate, about 5 lakh children die of diarrhoea every year.

The number of landless households in rural India is increasing day-by-day. Two decades ago,of every hundred families, 31 were landless. Today, the figure has increased to 41. This is a huge number,more than the population of many countries. There is little wage work available in rural India. Mechanisation, changes in crop patterns, continuous periods of drought, floods, increase in non-cultivation of agricultural land because of distress of the farmers have reduced the available days of agricultural work to on an average 50 per year in many parts of the country. In India, the adult labour force is estimated to be 400 million. The numbers for child labour are just guesses, but at the higher end they touch 100 million. So the actual labour force is close to 500 million or just 50 percent of our population. More than 60 percent of the labour force is unemployed or suffering from 'disguised unemployment'.

The Tenth Five Year Plan (2002-2007) had assumed that Indian agriculture production would grow by 4 percent per year. But the reality is that in the first three years of the Plan, agriculture could not even achieve 1.5 per cent rate of growth. The situation on the ground is alarming. Around 10 percent of India's farming households are landless. Another 67 percent own less than one hectare of land each. Eleven percent have 1-2 hectares of land. Yields have been stagnant. Irrigation facilities remain inadequate. Level of mechanisation is very low. Application of farm inputs is still inadequate. Therefore, if India has to grow by 7-8 percent per annum, agriculture has to grow faster since about 75 percent of India's population still earn their livelihood directly or indirectly from it.

As per latest Forbes' billionaires' list, India has become 8th in the list of top 10 of the super rich club with 12 billionnaires who have a combined wealth of $ 61.3 billion. The Forbes' billionaire club is a reflection of the way in which wealth is generated and distributed in India. The 12 Indian billionaires are together worth $61.3 billion–the average Indian billionaire's wealth is nine million times more than the average Indian person's worth in terms of per capita GDP. To expect that wealth will trickle down from rich to the poor and in the course of time bridge the income divide is to be naive. Disparities in wealth have to be addressed sincerely and require proactive steps on the part of the corporate sector, and the state–including the civil society.

As per the latest World Wealth Report of Merril Lynch, in India individuals with net worth of more than $ 1million have risen from 61,000 to 70,000 in 2004. India accounts for more than 10% of the 600,000 new millionaires who came up in 2004. The rate of increase of millionaires in India is far above the world average 7 percent. However, just one in 15,000 Indians is a millionaire, against one in 100 in the US. Across the world, there are 8.3 million members who are part of the million dollar club. If they pool their assets, their combined wealth would be $30.8 trillion which can easily buy a country.

What this statistics indicates – general economic prosperity or a growing inequility within and across countries. The UN's annual human development report for 2002 showed that during the 1990s, living standards actually fell in 50 countries. About 0.01% of world population are millionaire and 0.007% of Indian population are millionaire. If we consider this as the indicator of socio-economic value creation or prosperity, then we have to redefine the meaning of stupidity and hypocrisy.

What is the use of the so-called genius/talented management gurus,economists or intellectuals if they can't solve the basic problems of a vast majority of population ?How will the corporate sector be able to expand its market in a sustained manner if the vast majority of the population remains unemployed? If we are really interested in bringing the vast majority of people under the 'market net',we have to introspect and re-visit business models or strategies and focus our attention on the following:

- How to convert poor people into customers.
- How to create alternative options and choices for the vast majority of people.
- How to create the product/services which can help to improve and change the lifestyle of the poor people.

- How to engage the vast majority of people in productive economic activities to generate incomes.
- Income generation for the vast majority of people is the key driving force for social transformation giving dignity, hope and confidence to a vastly marginalised people.

In India, several rich people do not pay tax. Taxpayers who reported an income over Rs.10 lakh numbered only about 70000 in 2002-2003, according to the Kelkar Task Force on Direct Tax. According to a survey by the National Council of Applied Economic Research, the number of households with an annual income higher than Rs.10 lakh was already 08 lakh in 2001-2002, of which less than 9% of them filed an income tax return. How then can we expect social trust towards business or wealth creation?

Thus, on the one hand, there are 'competetive extravagant lifestyles' on the part of a few and unacceptable poverty on the part of majority of population- which is bound to increase social friction and contradiction, leading to a crisis of unmanageable dimensions. What is the relevence of big business houses, visionary leaders or CEOs? Why should the society bother or respect the business or corporate community?

All socio-economic activities have to be focussed on people. Only by doing this, social trust be achieved and social friction and contradiction be minimised to as acceptable level. Trust and respect are founded on the principles of knowledge, integrity and a real contribution to society. Trust gained through such activities will become the most invisible critical asset to survive in 21st century business and social environment.

The need of the hour is to transform the 'corporate character'. Corporate character should be free of intellectual hyprocrisy, myopia and superficial understanding. Corporate character is shaped, influenced and directed by core values and collective mind of the organisation like a human being is conditioned by the dynamics of the human mind and value system.

Corporate character is the invisible part of the organisation. Economic, commercial and other activities (processes) are the visible parts. Corporate character can be considered as the 'Base' and economic, commercial & other activities as the 'superstructure'. Both have to be synchronised in a manner to create socio-economic value. To achieve this the corporate character is required to be transformed, developed and nurtured to create the appropriate context for the organisation.

It is tried to define various aspects and attributes of the corporate character and its significance in the context of value creation and institution- building.Also an attempt is made to define 'what is socio-economic value' and its implications in respect of society and organisation.

Socio-economic value creation is the fundamental issue. This has to be understood, practised and propagated. A paradigm shift is required from the shareholder's or promoter's value maximization to the socio-economic value or surplus creation for the benefit of the society.

Without transforming the corporate character, an institution cannot be built. We will remain prisoners to the shareholders' value maximization **mirage or trap**. Organisations urgently should start to revisit and re-evaluate their managerial skills, strategy, policy mix and other activities to reorient themselves beyond bottomline and shareholders' value mind- set.

The whole purpose of this book is to impress the whole corporate and business community towards sincere 'introspection' and acceptance that socio-economic value creation or provision **product/services with socio-economic insight** is the key driving force.

In the 21st century, product or services have to be offered with socio-economic solutions. This is essentially required for the survival of corporation and also for respect and trust from the society. Organisation has to become the partner of society in a real sense. Social trust is itself a critical asset which has to be appreciated by the corporate or business community sincerely.

To achieve this, the 'balancesheet context' is required to be replaced by the 'socio-economic value' creation context through transforming the organisation 'mind wealth'. Corporate mind wellness is the key driving force for socio-economic value creation. Business relationships should be mainly based on socio-economic value nexus instead of money nexus.

A corporate body needs a heart. Archie W. Dunham, CEO, Conoco, said: "Strong financial results cannot be separated from corporate citizenship and that such corporate citizenship should be directed by the passion of its employees."

There is absolutely no intention to negatively challenge or criticise any theory/concept/idea of management thinkers/writers. The intention is to initiate re-thinking in our whole approach towards core values, socio-economic value creation and managing the corporations and enterprises in that direction.

Nothing is absolute in this world. Everything is in a relative state and in the process of continuous change or flux. Hence, we should sincerely follow the 'theory-practice-theory' approach. We should start with theory, go for practice and change or revise our theory within the context of reality. Theories, concepts and ideas are subject to obsolescence; Creativity and innovation are not. The creative mind is a critical asset since it appreciates value constantly. We should not be too possessive or dogmatic of our ideas or creation.

Market or reality is neutral. It does not depend on the egos of any individual. If we really are interested in social good, there should be a genuine dialogue among the practitioners of management and economic theories. As Danny Hills, inventor and a Disney fellow, rightly captured: "We have a world that has enough resources for everybody to live a very high standard of living and participate in a very productive vital economy. I think our responsibility is to move in directions that help us to do that as quickly as possible."

I sincerely believe in values, ethics, honesty and truth and it is this attitude that has given me the mental strength to dare write this book. I am aware that I am also very much part of the corporate reality. However, I cannot deal with the numerous sophisticated lies that people have started accepting as an integral part of corporate process or environment. I cannot accept the refined hypocrisy practiced by the so-called corporate leaders or intellectuals day in and day out. I donot want to be immune to the poverty, squalor, unhappiness, manipulation and corruption in the society. I don't want to pretend to close my eyes to such bold and bare truths of society. These black truths continuously haunt me and I was compelled to start thinking and the result is this small attempt.

I am aware that all this may not be appreciated and may be considered as abstract,intangible or irrelevant. But, I can't help it-this is my belief and this is my reality–since I sincerely believe: "Human problems cannot be solved by mere intellectual energy. Some of the cleverest criminals are intellectuals" said Swami Ranganathananda. This has been the genesis of my writing this book.

I do not dare to claim that I have invented or discovered a new concept or theory or jargon. All the concepts or ideas which are discussed in this book are already available in one form or the other. My only objective is to consolidate and give some sort of concrete shape to those ideas or concepts and appeal to all concerned through this book to introspect and shift the focus to *Corporate Character* in order to contribute for social good and well-being.

Through this book I would appeal to one and all would give their feedback, suggestion and criticism which will be of great help to modify, revise and refine the next version/edition.

I shall be extremely happy if this small attempt can contribute in any manner to propagate the significance of values and social good since I strongly believe in the teaching of a Chinese proverb:" The tree which fills the arms grew from the tiniest sprout; the tower of nine storeys rose from a small heap of earth; the journey of a thousand miles commenced with a single step."

Anup Kumar Mandal

Acknowledgements

No one was ever really taught by another; each of us has to teach himself. The external teacher offers only the suggestion which rouses the internal teacher to work to understand things.-

Swami Viveknanda

I cannot teach anybody anything, I can only make them think-

Socrates

I express my gratitude to one and all whose books,articles, write-ups, reports I have read/consulted to clarify ideas/ concepts, to conceptualise certain concepts and to give concrete shape to my ideas. Also in some cases, I have liberally used the content of some of the articles and topics to validate and enrich my ideas and also to bring clarity. It is practically impossible to thank individually all whose books, articles, write-ups, reports, personal discussions and other inputs or materials which I have consulted, referred or used in writing this book.

I am also greateful to my sweet daughter-Arpita and my caring & loving wife-Aparna who are my genuine critiques, well wishers, best friends and also sometimes playing the role of my parents. Without their sincere support and co-operation it would not have been possible for me to devote myself to writing this book.

Contents

1

Skeleton of Reality

The world is indeed a mixture of truth and make-believe. Discard the make-believe and take the truth

Sri Ramakrishna Paramahansa

Good ideas are not adopted automatically. They must be driven into practice with courageous patience

Hyman Rickover

Truth from facts

Theories and dogmas do not work in reality; we have to remove our sunglasses to see a more complete picture of reality, as Deng Xiaoping had once said; ' we have to learn truth from the facts.'

All over the world, corporate sector is facing serious challenges. Several companies are struggling to survive, several companies have closed their shops, several companies were declared bankrupt, several companies are involved in serious corruption/scandal, several companies are stagnant and are not able to grow further. This is true for both private and public enterprises.

Mega financial scandals that impact investors and other people worldwide like the Enron affair and the brazen way in which Union Carbide handled the human tragedy at Bhopal are only cases in point. For every known Enron and Union Carbide,there could be thousands of others whose misdemeanours remain unknown to the general public.

In several cases, employees and general public had to pay a huge price due to gross inefficiency and mismanagement in many companies. A recent example: Bankrupt British carmaker MG Rover finally collapsed on 15th April' 05 as administrators said there was no prospect of selling the business as a whole. Administrators Pricewaterhouse Coopers, appointed during the first week of April' 05, after a rescue deal with Shanghai Automative Industry Corp (SAIC) broke down, said there was no hope of saving the firm and that its 6,000 workers faced redundancy.

In the wake of allegations that the car group's saviours profited at the expense of the company's long-term survival, the UK government has set up an enquiry. The government has ordered an independent inquiry into the finances of MG Rover that collapsed with the loss of 6,000 jobs. The probe will be led by Sir Bryan Nicholson, chairman of the Financial Reporting Council, and carried out under its auspices. Nicholson will examine the accounts of all companies associated with Rover, including those of Phoenix Venture Holdings, its parent group, and go back five years to when Phoenix bought Rover for a mere £10m.

Corporate sector/business community either is involved in corruption/manipulation or tolerating and indirectly encouraging it. As per a newspaper report, India is still a lowly 90th on the Graft Index (CPI-Corruption Perception Index). More than a decade of reforms has not helped India shake off the perception that it is amongst the most corrupt business environments.

India has been ranked a lowly 90 in the total of 145 countries which were evaluated by Transparency

International(TI), a transnational NGO spearheading the anti-graft fight. India scored just 2.8 points out of 10 on honesty. As per TI, the Indian taxpayer loses a whopping $7 billion per year in bribery and a slew of scandals.

It seems that all their highly paid strategists and policy makers of companies are not able to figure out the problem or the reason for crisis. Some excellent companies of yesterday become the worst companies today like Enron and World Com. Lot of margers and acquisitions are taking place to survive and grow. Everybody knows the story of Home Trade Ltd. and its CEO.

Recently, the Global Trust Bank has become the biggest 'distrust' Bank having a large bad debt Rs.1200 crore at the cost of innocent depositors. Review reports of some of the major accounts of GTB by the audit and consulting firm Ernst & Young in 2001 had clearly pointed out how funds to loan accounts of some of the companies were diverted to a number of Ketan Parekh group entities. In doing so, GTB officials had flouted several norms laid down by the Reserve Bank Of India (RBI). The Ernst & Young report found that disbursals were made to some companies despite several of the loan proposals being incomplete, and in violation of the group exposure norms stipulated by the RBI. The loans were proposed, recommended and sanctioned without any stipulation for security, even though the amount involved was more than 50% of the net worth of the bank.

In March 2001, the Rs 2100 crore Madhavpura Mercantile Co-operative Bank collapsed under the weight of Rs 1200 crore of bad loans it made to Ketan Parekh and his cronies. A study by All India Bank Employees Association reveals that as of 31 March 2001, a total of 12090 accounts have defaulted Rs.80246. 46 crore due to banks and financial institutions. As per the All India Bank Employees Association report published during March 2005, about Rs. 3,00,000 crore out of total deposit of Rs. 15,00,000 crore were non-performing assets (NPAs), most of which had been written off. List of defaulters suggested that the major ones were all big companies:

1. Malavika Steels-Rs.1227 crore.
2. Modern Syntex-Rs.867 crore.
3. Prakash Industries-Rs.725 crore.
4. Llyods Steel India-Rs.595 crore.
5. Usha Ispat -Rs.555 crore.
6. Balaji Hotels-Rs 477 crore.
7. Mafatlal Industries-Rs.440 crore.
8. Hindustan Photo Films-Rs.422 crore.
9. DCM-Rs.372 crore.
10. J.K.Synthetics-Rs.352 crore.

On 3 December, 2004 the licence of the Hydrabad-based Prudential Cooperative Bank was finally cancelled by the regulator, the RBI–after two years of liquidity crunches, defaults and runs by depositors. The closure of the bank, which had 182,000 depositors, is the second biggest failure since the failure of Madhavpura Mercantile Cooperative Bank. The Prudential Bank's failure once again exposed how nakedly a few powerful defaulters have managed to destroy an 80-year old bank within a decade. In All likelihood, defaulters would get away without paying their dues. Once again, the deposit insurance fund will be used to bail out depositors.

We know the gross failure of UTI to manage the US-64 scheme. US-64 was the first mutual fund launched in the country by UTI in 1964. At the time of termination, it had over two crores investors with unit capital of around Rs.11500 crore. Many small investors included pensioners who had put their life's savings into the fund in the belief that it was virtually underwritten by the government and hence secure. What they got back was not even their capital.

The first signs of US-64's faltering health were detected in 1999. In June that year, the government bought out all PSU stocks in the portfolio of US-64 for Rs.3,300 crore, although their market value was only about Rs.1,516 crore. The scheme was suffering with a huge mismatch in underlying assets and liabilities because of fall in stock markets. Finally ordinary investors got peanut returns when the scheme was terminated in May, 2003.

In the stock market also, there is a crisis of trust and credibility. As per RBI's annual report, the percentage of financial savings of the household sector, invested to shares and debentures, has decreased drastically to 1.4% of total financial savings in 2003-04, from 7.7% in 1999-2000. The households have been exibiting reticence at a time when the markets have been booming, but it does reflect the reality that, unlike the sensex, investor confidence in the markets is nowhere near the peak. Sound capital markets must have a large and active individual investor base. They add to the numbers, leading to better price discovery and serve as a counterweight to large powerful investors as FIIs who influence the course of the market. Individual investors do not have the trust and confidence in the system. Recurrent scams, price volatility,fraudulent company managements and poor corporate governance have all contributed to the diminishing faith of the individual investor in the stock market.

The problem is clearly illustrated in a study conducted by the Society for Capital Market Reasearch & Development. As per the study, in 2002, almost 40% of the investors surveyed listed volatility and price manipulation as the main reasons for the diminishing confidence level.

Several stock market manipulations and insider trading scandals in India and abroad were published during the last decade. But still it is happening and the latest insider trading scandal in the New York Stock Exchange has been unearthed, if the newspaper report is to be believed. Fifteen specialists who managed trades on the floor of the New York Stock Exchange(NYSE) used their inside positions to earn an estimated $20million in illicit gains for themselves and their firms, federal authorities charged on Tuesday. The Securities and Exchanges Commission also filed civil charges against 20 specialists, including the 15 charged in the criminal indictment, and the NYSE as well. Federal authorities said that between 1999 and mid 2003, specialists at five firms put their companies' orders ahead of customers' orders, causing those customers to get inferior prices on a scheme the NYSE 's internal regulators failed to catch.

Hence, it is quite natural that average investors are losing faith day-by-day in the stock market process.

As per a recent newspaper report, six marketing heads were changed in seven years in one of the best known companies. There is also an article recently published in a business magazine-about remaking of one of the famous and giant FMCG companies. The company is literally struggling to protect its bottomline and achieve some growth. They have taken several initiatives: organisational restructuring, new model for diversification/growth, new brand management strategy, product positioning strategy, pricing strategy and strategy to counter competition. It seems nothing is working as desired. Nobody seems to be able to comprehend the real disease; but only trying to address the symptoms desperately.

The article as published in itself proves that the 'company brand' or 'product brand' is no longer the key driving force and the so-called CEOs have become paper tigers as Jay Lorsch, Professor of Human Relations at Harvard Business

School rightly said: "I think the CEO is over-rated. I am not saying CEO's are not important, don't get me wrong. It's a sickness that we have got. Their importance is way overstated."

As per a newspaper report, disgruntled investors blasted Daimler Chrysler Chief Executive Juergen Schrempp and top managers on 06th April 2005 for what they called poor performance and shoddy leadership at the world's fifth biggest carmaker. At a marathon annual meeting, shareholders lined up to complain about a series of problems capped last week by the automaker's biggest ever car recall and news of hefty charges to restructure its loss -making Smart minicar brand.

"The shareholders' patience is exhausted,"said Klaus Kaldemorgen from German fund manager DWS, scoffing at Schrempp's self-proclaimed ability to master situations. "Do you have to shoot yourslef in the foot first to provide first-aid?" he asked, complaining that the company had thoughtlessly put its flagship Mercedes brand at risk by letting the quality lag badly. "Playing down results seems to have become part of the corporate culture." he said to applause. "The problems at the Mercedes and Smart suggest serious management mistakes," said Thomas Maier at Union Investment, administrator of Daimler Chrysler shares worth $644 million.

Consultants are making huge money out of this confusion and chaos. Several investment plans or capital allocation models are being drawn and redrawn. Lot of marketing segmentation, branding, penetration, pricing, promotion and advertisement strategies are drawn and redrawn but it seems nothing is working. Recent examples are that some of the best known FMCG companies are struggling and desperately trying to outsmart the competitors by a price war to survive and grow. One wonders what is happening. Consulting firms are having good business by creating expectation by their elitist models, matrix or equations.

Vinoy Kamat in his article 'Instinctive Corporation' mentioned: "Whatever their strategic rationale, firms are very much like people. They are fashion-conscious, embracing every new management fad that debuts on global corporate catwalks. Trends are sampled, savoured and structured at great cost. Yet, most management fads have failed to create flexible organizations that react to the environment instinctively."

We have to really become sincere by removing our elitist ego, and do try to understand some of the fundamental truths which are quite simple. No complicated model is required to understand those. All these are happening because of an inappropriate 'organisation mind' or 'corporate character'' Organisation mind has to be transformed if we really want to change the situation', and the process of transformation should start earnestly.

Like the human mind, organization mind is the invisible power that organises and creates the context and dynamism for utilisation of an organisation's resources and people. Without a proper mind no human being can achieve and contribute, similarly no organization can contribute for social good without proper mind dynamics. Swami Vivekananda had once observed: "No great work can be achieved by humbug. It is through love, a passion for truth, and tremendous energy, that all undertakings are accomplished." He also said: "Respect the human being the human being is above everything."

Human being is the key as Zig Zigler rightly mentioned: "Sophisticated technology solves process problems, but we need that human being to demonstrate its effectiveness."

Mata Amritanandamayi said:".... finally everything is in the power of intention (mind). Today if our society is pervaded by fear, greed, rage, stress, drinks, drugs, rape, abuse, and hopelessness, it's because our intentions center on ego needs.

But if our intentions are aimed inside, towards God, towards service, towards giving, a safe and happy society cannot be far away".

Several management gurus and thinkers including the great Peter Drucker have started realizing the power and importance of the mind and human being for survival of the corporations. They are giving new definitions and interpretations to management theories which is in essence what some social thinkers like Swami Vivekananda have already propagated. Their new approach is mainly centered around the following main aspects:

- Respecting creativity of people
- Value system
- Profit to non -profit approach or mindset
- Low cost options or choices for majority population
- CSR–Corporate Social Responsibility

If we analyse in detail these are nothing but accepting that value is created by people, around people and for the people, Whether we take the Marxist point of view, Amartya Sen's Welfare Economics, C.K.Prahalad's Bottom Of Pyramid or Peter Drucker's Non-profit approach, or Swami Vivekananda's social philosophy, three basic issues will always be central to all socio-economic activities and value generation:

1. Humanity/Humanism–people are greater than profit

Humanism is the key driving force. Only humanism can bring the real social transformation. Baba Amte was quite right when he suggested in a recent interview: "All isms are almost lying on the death bed including Gandhism. Only ism is consumerism which presently exists in the world. So consumerism decides the price of man and not his value. Creative humanism alone will inspire the youth of the world because affluence has brought a lot of boredom in rich countries."

2. Value/surplus creation

Value is created in any sector–agriculture, manufacturing & service—by the people and that is a result of their mind-work and creativity. The issue is how to utilise the potential of human beings to create socio-economic value in a sustained manner.

3. Distribution of surplus or value:

Patterns and mechanism of distribution of value are also decided by the people. The main issue is how to bring equity in the distribution process of value to reduce social conflicts and disharmony.

The so-called factors of production/services like land, labour, capital, technology, knowledge etc. will be useless unless a proper guiding force and integration cord is available, and which is nothing but the 'character' of the company. 'Corporate Character' can only create the 'context' for socio-economic value creation.

Without integrity of management, operational effeciency is of no use. We should remember 'Crooked managements are like leaking tyres.' They can not contribute in institution building. The competitive edge of any company will be decided by the quality of corporate character, and not by any other factor. The potential of technology and talent cannot be utilised, developed, cherished or nurtured without a proper corporate character.

'Corporate character' is not a factor of production, or input, which is available off the shelf in the market, neither it is available on loan from a bank nor acquired from consultancy firms. Moreover, ethics, commitment, conviction, inspiration, creativity, compassion etc which are the basics of character can not be automised or programmed even by the best software or computer in the world. These are to be collectively appreciated, developed, practised and nurtured.

In short, institution is a sum total of truthfulness, trust, transparency, team, talent, technology, transformation and transmutation of values.

'Customer is King'–No Longer Relevant

'Customer is king'-this concept cannot motivate and move the whole organisation for socio-economic value creation. Somehow the interpretation is 'to manage the customer. 'Experts and consultants have formulated and reformulated several jargons and so-called customer-centric concepts, but without much success. Some notable jargons are:

- Customer care
- Customer suggestion scheme
- Customer relationship management
- Customer satisfaction mapping/index
- Customer cell
- Customer value data/index
- Observation of customer year
- Customer should be delighted
- Customer value management
- ROC–Return on Customer
- Customer delight index
- Customer loyality index
- Customer dissatisfaction index
- Customer experiential management

In reality, all these concepts ideas have become bureaucratic rituals or formalities without any real significance. Either one or two departments or a few people are involved to care about the customers.

According to an international study of customer service attitudes in 19 countries, while 60% regarded customers in a positive way, 40% had either neutral or outright negative feelings towards customers. Further, the study discovered that as work pressure increased so did the negative responses.

As per another study, quality of after sales service in India at best was described as average. Even the largest durable companies in India were way below the global benchmark of allocating upto 2% of their revenues to after-sales service. As per the study, overall quality of after sales service was averaged 45-50% based on the following parameters:

- Ease of access to service centre
- Time taken to respond
- Convenience of time fixed for repair
- Courtesy and patience shown
- Resolving problem on first visit
- Advice provided on other needs
- Accuracy of estimate to actual cost

In the rural and semi-urban markets in particular, non-availability of spares causes tremendous customer dissatisfaction because the customers have to travel a long distance from their residence to the dealers'place for repair. Most of the companies have devoted little resources to after-sales service and their main priority have been sales growth. In the bargain customers are taken for a ride. However, good customer service can be ensured if we remove the superficial slogan'customer is king' but genuinely believe that the company exists because of customers.

'Customer is king' implies that the focus is on how to manage the customer not the socio-economic value creation. Hence a corporation is busy in targeting customers, marketing segmentation strategy and aligning the product and services accordingly. If wine, tobacco, cosmetic, pornography, sex, adult movies or entertainment can manage the target customer, there is no hesitation to adopt a strategy even with a negative implication for the society.

In most of the companies 'customer satisfaction' is the responsibility of either one or two departments though people may claim that all are responsible. Unless the whole organisation is aligned to create extraordinary experience and value creation for customers, 'customer is king' will remain a joke or at best an advertising campaign material.

To build the 'institution', socio-economic value creation should be the focus or the centre of all activities.

Is Annual Report Significant?

The annual report card does not reflect the socio-economic value creation details. It is almost impossible to understand the contribution of the company towards socio-economic value creation from the annual report. Moreover, it is impossible to understand the quality of corporate character from the annual report.

Annual reports are published on a yearly basis. The annual report is supposed to provide a complete picture of a company's performance/activities in the previous financial year.

Most of the companies are investing a huge amount of money on design and content of the Annual Report through choosing themes, commissioning design houses and copywriters, using glossy paper, doing layouts that are attractive and catchy. But the real question is what they reveal and what they conceal–mostly they conceal more than they reveal.

The Department of Company affairs (DCA) and the Institute Of Chartered Accountants Of India (ICAI) have specified a standard format for annual reports and some minimum disclosure norms for companies to follow. However, a company is free to share more information/data on various business activities/aspects if it considers them important. But very few companies in reality do that. In general, different aspects of an Annual report are:

- The Balance Sheet
- The Profit and Loss account
- Notes on accounts
- Statement of cashflows
- Subsidiary performance
- Governance report

Performance in terms of ethical practices/social resposibility or socio-economic value creation is rarely mentioned in the Annual Report. Socio-economic value creation and quality of corporate character are not being evaluated at all.

If any company really wants to become an institution it has to eliminate the 'Balancesheet Syndrome'. That financial and physical performance are the yardsticks to measure the success of any commercial organisation; is superficial old thinking. There are other aspects beyond the BalanceSheet which need to be seriously considered like obligation towards society, the environment in which it operates, ethical aspects etc.

Without the disclosure of performance in respect of social good, there is no basis for evaluating corporate contribution towards responsible business practice. Ritu Kumar rightly observed in an article 'Corporate Philanthropy': "...Another broader measure of corporate commitment to social responsibility is the UN Global Compact, a set of 10 principles launched by the UN Secretary General Kofi Annan. Currently, 95 Indian companies have backed the Global Compact.......One quick indicator: of the 95 supporters of the Global Compact from corporate India, only one Atlas Cycles–has produced the annual communication on progress that is expected of the compact's supporters. And while most large corporations now disclose some information on their social or environmental programmes-with Bhel, Dr. Reddy's, HLL and Tisco in the vanguard–much remains highly descriptive and qualitative, lacking the rigour of common, quantified performance information that characterises company financial accounts. Companies routinely claim that their employees are their greatest asset-yet provide little evidence how this asset is being valued and enhanced..."

Human Resource Management- Is it Really working?

In reality it is not working. Without a proper corporate character 'HR' becomes merely a term on paper. Still only 35-40 % of the employee's ability is being utilized as per various studies already conducted, and the proper 'unlocking of employees potential' still remains a distant dream. The hard reality is–

- In most of the cases the core group does not have much faith in HR. Ultimately it depends on the whims and fancies of the core group and personal agendas of the individuals.
- In most of the companies HR department works like the personnel & administrative department.
- There is a huge disconnect between business strategy or perspective and HR.
- On paper, mouthful of theories jargons are mentioned, yet in practice it is the promoters/CEOs or few top

management people who decide the policy, procedure and practices of HR as per their whims and fancies.

- In some of the companies it has been observed that within a span of 5 years 4/5 HR heads were being replaced or had resigned. If HR heads are themselves not able to continue, how is the HR department to facilitate the development and retention of employees?
- In several companies, the reality is that bureaucracy, feudal approach, ad hoc policy, personal likes, dislikes, favouritism, the issue of connected people being given undue advantages and internal politics decide most of the things. Moreover, convenient definitions are being invented to justify anti-HR practices and policies also.
- Boss-subordinate conflicts create confusion and frustration. Still most of the companies are run by orders, notes dictates of the bosses. There is hardly any real communication, consultation or dialogue.
- The Annual Performance appraisals are rituals to be followed. At the end of the year a performance appraisal exercise cannot make any real contribution in employee development and improvement of the performance.
- There is a feeling that no boss/top management is genuinely interested in getting the feedback. Most of the company does not work on merit alone, there are always prejudices at work.
- There is no real concern for the people. There is no transparent and equitable distribution of information. Top management people are not at all accessible or lack openness.
- Several companies' HR heads are not competent or sincere in contributing for full utilization of the potential of the people or do not have the context to do so.

- Several HR firms or HR consulting firms are themselves suffering from HR problems and struggling to retain people or experiencing dissatisfation of employees.
- In most of the cases the core group of the organisation suffers from 'outsider syndrome'–they value knowledge possessed by outsiders more than the knowledge possessed by employees and indirectly discourage internal innovation and the use of potential. Hence consultants are making easy money.

Unless the corporate character is transformed and employees are really considered as the 'Internal Customers', nothing will work in reality.

One of the top executives from a big Advertising agency who resigned, expressed his unhappiness thus:"......(I am) tired the way Agency treated its people. There was always immense pressures from the head office on meeting targets. Agencies across the board are concerned with profits and take ad hoc decisions to prop up the bottomline. They do not invest in people, and pay poorly. They have forgotten that profits follow if they focus on their people, culture, personality and processes." Unfortunately, this is true to a great extent for most of the companies.

Mercer, a consulting firm successfully completed a unique HR Transformation Survey across the Asian market place in 2003. The report stressed that the HR function of the future must be successful in four distinct roles:

- As a strategic business partner
- Change agent
- Employee champion
- Administrative expert

Company cultures tend to be either very externally focussed, flexible and adaptable with market needs. Or they can be more internally focussed, where policies, rules and procedures tend to dominate and where efficiency is rewarded. The issue is how to manage efficiency and innovation for creating socio-economic value and get competitive advantage by making differentiation in the market place. This is leadership and is context-driven not HR driven. The HR cannot fill for mediocrity anywhere in the organisation. HR is as good as the organisation.

The real issue boils down ultimately to corporate character. Unless context is created HR is irrelevant or at the most useful for administrative purposes only. Recently, Wayne Peat, Regional Human Capital Leader, IBM Business Consulting Services, candidly mentioned in an interview: "Today, HR is not as well connected as it should be with business. HR is fabulous at doing the work of a personal administrator, for making sure that organisations comply with the letter of the law. But the concept of becoming a provider of value-adding services to the business, of becoming a business partner that understands where the organisation is going, or even to take a leadership position–so that it can justifiably sit at the board table with the CEO and the board of directors and chart new directions for the organisation–is sadly lacking."

Employees Get the Last Preference

In reality, the employee is considered less important when a facility or a benefit is given. We have seen that even for cost cutting measures the employee is being targetted first. As per a recent *Economic Times* study, it is clear that at ground reality the employee is given the last preference.

By and large the study shows the following preference equation:

- Director -shareholder-employees or
- Share holder-director-employees.

Average percentage growth for the last four years.
(Figs taken from Economic Times, 29 Sept, 04)

Comapny	Employee	Directors' remuneration	Dividend
Cipla	18.9	9335.2	49.4
TVS Motor	28.05	796.16	19.7
Arvind Mills	19.68	318.33	0
Godrej Indus	1.57	111.71	44.51
Apollo Tyres	11.46	83.52	06
Grasim	4.97	76.4	21.2
Essar Steel	30.74	64.08	0
Infosys	49.06	19.27	172.5
Satyam	27.85	(-)10.2	967.3
ABB	4.61	10.15	7.59

Figure: 1 Percentage growth of remuneration/cost

Main observations made by the study are:

- In most manufacturing firms, directors' remuneration have multiplied several times in the last four financial years.
- Employees have last preference–either director-shareholder-employees or shareholder-director-employees is the basic preference equation.

- In no company is an employee given the first preference
- The gap between the employees and the directors is too high
- In a number of cases, a good chunk of shares are held by the promoters who double up as directors and so they are ranking in a much bigger sum of money.

Many surveys or feedback systems have been introduced in various companies like employee satisfaction surveys, employee perception surveys, employee attitude surveys, 360 degree feedback system etc. But in reality in most of the cases it is not giving the desired results since the proper context is missing.

All the surveys/feedback systems are directly proportionate to the quality of trust an organisation can inspire among its employees. The effectiveness of surveys/feedback systems depends on the quality of an open and transparent context and the sincerity of the core people.

Are CEOs Overrated?

If we look into the last 50 years of corporate history, so many CEOs failed to deliver, so many CEOs were sacked, so many CEOs were involved in corporate mis conduct, and so many others were involved in scandals. In the wake of Enron and World Com, the myth of the Charismatic CEO lies shattered. Recently in India, GTB collapsed. Even Hindustan Lever is struggling to grow and protect its bottomline.

There were several CEOs who were reported to be involved in corporate mis-conduct, fraudulant activities and were proved as just white collar crooks. A latest example: As per a newspaper report, the Chief Executive behind Australia's largest corporate collapse, Ray Williams, was jailed for four years on 15.04.05 after he pleaded guilty in Dec '04 to three counts stemming from his management of HIH from 1998 to 2000.

Mr. Rakesh Khurana, Assistant Professor at Harvard Business School, rightly said: "Charismatc CEOs are not what companies need. However, it has become a dangerous corporate obssession for companies to turn to these types in the hope that they will save the firm. Charisma is not a bad thing, but charismatic authority is of the worst kind. There are no messiahs , and this is important for CEOs and the public to realize".

In reality, CEO charisma is not related to better performance but to higher salaries for the CEO. In a recent interview, Rosabeth Moss Kanter, Professor, Harvard Business School stated: "We have certainly created a cult of celebrity CEOs when they don't deserve it, though, in a turnaround leadership does matter because people are floundering and looking for a leader. But to create success, that leader must produce more leaders. It sometimes happens automatically when a leader puts in a culture where he encourages initiative."

Success or failure of any organisation is too complex an issue to be analysed in reference to one or two individuals. Individual brilliance is important but not sufficient to face the complex and uncertain dynamic situations and challenges i.e., in terms of technology changes, socio-economic development, changes in customer preferences, domestic political uncertainties, competitors innovativeness, financial market fluctuations, statutory changes or international etc.

Another problem most of the CEOs are facing is the isolation and non-connection from the reality and the organisation. Daniel Goleman observed: "The CEO disease has to do with the fact that the higher you go in the leadership ladder the less honest people will be with you. Because people become fearful, for example, they don't want to bring bad news. They don't want to tell you things which will upset you for fear that you will get upset with them, which unfortunately, and too often, happens. So people keep quiet. It means that the person at the top of the organisation, who theoretically should know the most, very often knows the least or is the last to find out. That means that leaders, to be effective, have to be proactive in getting information. They have to be active in setting a tone or creating a culture where people can be candid."

This basically means that corporate character is the key driving force and not any individual. Corporate character is required to be transformed to create the right context to the CEO to contribute for the effectiveness of the organisation.

The Mind of "A Balancesheet" Company

A "Balancesheet" company does not believe that value is created by people, around people and for the people. They do not give much importance to organizations, mind transformation or utilization. Their core value/purpose is shareholder value maximization. Their main points of concentration/attention are:

- Market capitalization/shareholders' value
- Profit & loss account–bottom line maximisation
- Charisma/intelligence of CEO/promoters
- Market share
- Marketing strategy/advertising strategy
- Capital allocation model
- Managing the environment(read Government)
- Maximisation of top management or promoters' interest.

Balancesheet companies are suffering from two main syndromes:

- 'We- are- in -the -business- of -making -money' syndrome.
- 'Business- of- business- is- business'-syndrome

Central to all their activities is to maximize shareholders' value through CEOs or promoters. CEOs or promoters are the source and distributor of power, knowledge information. They are considered as sacrosanct and invincible, and ultimately greed becomes the invisible core value.

The Sensex (Stock/share price) is not a true indicator of a country's economic social health. Similarly this cannot reflect the real value creation by the corporation or organisation. Empirically/ historically it is proven that Stock market Index is not only a poor indicator of value creation or health of the company but sometimes it misleads also. There are economists management experts who have been trying their best to equate the value creation with the gyrations of the stock market to confuse the real issue.

The Stockmarket is basically a place for trading risks and speculation. If anybody loses from short-term swings, it is only those who have speculatively invested their wealth in the hope of quick gains. All the gains and loss are simply on paper and do not imply any erosion of the country's real wealth. Similarly it is true for an organisation. Even with very little change in the fundamentals of the economy/company stock, valuations were pushed up to an abnormal level due to factors other than fundamentals of the economy or the company.

It has been observed that in the 'price' of stock and the 'intrinsic value' of stock or the fundamentals of the company in value creation, there is no correlation. It generally depends on various extraneous factors which have nothing to do with the real value of the company.

On 17 May 2004 (Black Monday), intraday, the Sensex had crashed 842 points which forced the exchanges to close trading twice during the day. At close, the index was down 565 points, or 11%, the second highest single-day fall in the history of the market. How can one explain this incident? This fluctuation of the index has nothing to do with the health of the economy or corporate sector-this is the result of smart manipulation by some investors.

If the core value is shareholder value maximisation–no company can become an institution which creates socio-economic values. A Balancesheet company does not care about society or country. The objective is to make money and maximize profit. If pornography, brothels or strip business maximize profit, they will not hasitate to invest or diversify or to make a growth strategy in these businesses.

Recently there was a news item, that Australia's Daily Planet will concentrate or invest in Strip clubs since there is more money in owning a strip club than in owning brothel. Money is the determining factor not the people society. Subhabrata Ghosh, Executive Director and COO,

Saatchi & Saatchi candidly observed in an article : "Is it realistic to demand honesty from organisation?....most organisations are run by investors whose primary motive is to make money quickly. Every Windows edition is released with bugs. Carmakers produce unsafe cars. Drug companies make unsafe drugs. Remember thalidomide? There are so many drugs banned in the Western world. Why are they still marketed in India?"

Can Advertisement, Promotion or Brand Management save the Company?

The answer is NO. In today's very competitive and crowded situation, effectiveness of advertisement and promotion is very limited. Beyond a certain point, the value gotten out of advertising drops exponentially.

The so called innovative creation of many advertising firms could not improve market shares or create new markets for several companies. Even several of the top companies after spending crores of rupees on ad failed to protect their bottom line. In reality, all the so-called creativity of genius creative directors of ad agencies are proved to be nothing more than a lip service to maintain the 'brand'. Advertisement or promotion cannot ensure trust or loyalty of the consumers towards the brand.

There is a huge non-connection or superficiality in the whole approach of advertisement. Even the advertisement professionals already have started realising the futility of superficiality. Prasoon Joshi, Creative Director, McCann Erickson India observed candidly in an article:".... Or take the use of superlatives such as 'new' or 'best'. The client feels that he has 'said it all' with them, but is the consumer decoding them? More importantly, does the consumer believe these claims? Advertising, in trying to create hyperbole, has sounded the death knell of superlatives. We have managed to make them non-existent in the consumer's mind..... In the ad world, the language, the people, and the situations don't mirror society, nor does society mirror them. In the hope of becoming aspirational, we often make the mistake of alienating the consumer. Clients and creators need to understand that there is nothing more amazing, and relatable, like real life....we can sell in the most effective manner if we are able to connect with our consumers in their own world and not in some world of fantasy."

Promotional strategies like free gifts,discounts ,special offers have failed to create genuine demand. In most of the cases these promotional strategies have failed to sustain or develop market share. Customer loyalty can be achieved only by establishing the trust of the customer through continuous socio-economic value creation. No superficial activity will work in today's market-place.

There is a very high rate of product failure, as per one estimate,about 80 percent of new consumer products fail, about 30 percent busines-to-business offerings fail. Too many of the new products are simply copies of others instead of offering new value and benefits.

Branding strategy is not working in most of the cases. Several brands have met with untimely death. Several brands are struggling to survive. The essence of branding strategy has been shifted from the intrinsic value of products and services to a superficial value through the so-called creative advertisements and promotions. Most of the companies are interested in market capitalisation and profitability than to offer a real benefit to customers. In the bargain, advertising agencies are minting money by selling superficial ideas, catchy lines or content to impress customers as well as companies.

Consumers' real brand experience begins when they use the product or service. Marketing professionals/brand managers often forget that sustained competitive advantage can only come from better solutions to consumer needs and not by a smart 30 or 60-seconds TV commercial. Most of the Brand Managers do not have the complete in depth understanding of the various aspects of the products and the process to develop or manufacture the product. How many brand managers are really interested to spend their time in factories or R&D centre to understand the product? Monthly or quarterly targets also create pressure on executives to focus on quick fixes like manipulating price, pack size, ad budgets or giving away some free gifts-instead of the far harder task of developing consumer insights that can be used to create a value- added product.

Years of squeezing profits by trading quality for cost savings has resulted in 'me too' products that consumers are prepared to switch from, for a buck or free gift. Customers are really telling brand managers that their products have no genuine USP or superiority and hence, donot deserve their loyalty. The consumer is a distant reality for most of the company; only marketing and sales own the consumer, whereas it is absolutely necessary that everyone in the organisation should own the consumer.

A customer-centric organisation becomes a reality when all functions begin to understand their consumer based reality and work together to serve them. This transformation, often hard, can be done if the core leadership consistently demonstrates that no one wins unless customers win. Once internal barriers are broken and cooperation, collaboration, empowerment, mutual respect and free flow of information and ideas are unleashed, the most unexpected results can be achieved. In reality most of the companies are still product-centric as observed by Harvey Thompson in his book *'Who Stole My Customer?'*: "Very few companies are customer-centric–most are product-centric and it's there that the problem lies."

Due to an open information and communication system, exposure to internet, TV and other media, nobody is able to control or arbitrage information or knowledge-customers are more informed, knowledgeable and open to expriment and to new ideas, and have started demanding new options or choices.

Brand loyalty has become a myth. The company has to establish a delivery system to ensure creative product/services with better experience, choices, price options, conveniences and intrinsic value of the product. Purchasing decisions will be influenced by the above not the brand loyalty, and that's the reality. Hindustan Lever, Proctor & Gamble, Pepsi, Coke and many other companies are struggling to protect their market share. Recently Uniliver decided to reduce its number of brands from 1600 to 400 since keeping several brands is just a wastage of money and effort. This itself is the best example of brand loyalty being a myth.

There is confusion among the experts even regarding the effectiveness of the so called 'power brand'. Power branding is much of a rage among the FMCG marketers who are now under attack from regional brands and other low cost options available in the market place. Whether it is Hindustan Lever Ltd, Proctor & Gamble, Godrej Consumer Products or Dabur, accepted branding strategy is that it is good to have fewer and stronger brands rather than an entire line of smaller ones. The reasons generally cited are:

- High costs of advertisement
- Difficulty in focussing management attention and investment in smaller brands.

Hindustan Lever, the most powerful FMGC comapany, is also struggling to retain market share with its power brand. Now the company is in the process of revamping brands across its personal care portfolio to keep pace with low-priced competition, revive market share and pre-empt proposed launches by multinational rivals. Both the power brands-Liril, Lux and others are being overhauled by introduction of new variants, packaging and even formulations. Liril's market share has been stagnating at about 2.5% of the total soaps market for over two years. Lux's market share has remained at 15% over the last two years, and in fact, has declined 2-3% in the past four years.

There is a question mark in respect of the effectiveness of power brands. As per some experts it all depends on the level of heterogeneity in the market i.e the perception of the customers. If customers want different things from similar products, a power brand may not be that effective. Some experts are questioning the value of spending so much money on brand building and advertisement given the fact that many brands are fast moving towards commoditisation due to stiff price competition.

USP-Differentiation Confusion

Every organisation is trying desperately to offer some sort of USP (Unique Selling Proposition) or differentiation in product or service but consumers are not satisfied or responding postively. They can't perceive the differences. Superficial USP like free offers, gift scheme, lottery prize etc are launched/re-launched to attract the consumers and the same is copied by other companies.Competitive pricing, price cut, low price version are introduced/re-introduced. Companies are suffering from the 'me- too syndrome'.

For most organisations,consumers are statistics or data,based on which market segmentation is done, demand potentials calculated, investments made, products manufactured. But the fundamental question is why a particular product or a brand is purchased or preferred. Now we are in the age of product equality in all categories, an age of instant communication and high exposure of consumers to competitive advertisement and information explosion.

As Jack Trout observed, "Unfortunately, we currently have an epidemic of schizophrenia thanks to endless line extensions. A well-known research firm called Copernicus investigated 48 pairs of leading brands in 48 different product and service categories. The objective was to measure whether brands were becoming more similar and commodity-like over time. Of the 48 categories evaluated, 40 were perceived as becoming similar. The reason: a shift from brand building to promotional programmes, a shift from information-oriented advertising to entertainment-oriented advertising and a failure to communicate a distinctive point of difference.

All companies are having basically the same information, similar products/services, offer similar types of USPs or similar types of promotion or advertisements. In the 21st century market is dominated by similarity and plenty of phenomena. Old marketing theories of creating USP/differentiation is not working at all. We have entered the era of 'commoditisation'.

Fundamentals of marketing theories based on reality of old era where real differentiation/USP were existant. First mover advantage created giants. There were monopoly over information, technology, capital and marketing power.

Things have changed drastically. Ideas/capital/information/ knowledge is nobody's monopoly now. We have to reinvent those theories to come out from the 'me-too syndrome' to create genuine value for the customers. Purposeful creativity is required, not superficiality or imitation,and which, if continuous depends on ideas, imaginations and innovations.

Operational competencies and product innovations are both essential but not sufficient to differentiate a company in the market place. Organisation has to understand the customer's needs in a real sense which is possible only through creative thinking, interaction and dialogue with the customers and understand the socio-economic issues as existing in reality. Being market oriented, being customer oriented, we need to understand very clearly who the customer is? What are the customer's needs. Define these very clearly, across organisation, how we can create customer value? In the 21st century product/services are required to be offered with socio-economic solutions or insights. Purposeful creative thinking, therefore, is required to innovate product/services with socio-economic solutions.

In today's dynamic environment,customers have access to information and therefore a wide range of choices and very high expectations. Creating a meaningful differentiation and a unique brand experience in this environment is the most critical challenge for any company.

The starting point of any brand-building activity is the understanding of the evolving needs of the customer and putting in place a comprehensive customer feedback system which will help the organisation to continuously track questions like-who the current customers are, why are they buying from the company, are they satisfied with current offerings or do they need something else, etc. This should be the basis for any brand management process. The challenge for any brand is to keep pace with the evolving customer needs. The task of keeping the brand relevant to customers at all times requires commitment of a very high order across the organisation.

Only those companies will be able to survive in the long run which create value with socio-economic insights. For this all marketing tools/strategy/tactics have to be aligned and the whole organisation has to be a part of the collaborative effort. Traditional brand management/segmentation theory will not work any more.

Consultant no Panacea

Can a consultant bring transformation of the organisational mind which can the make organisation a socio-economic value creating institution? The answer is NO. Consultants are also in the business of selling ideas and making profit. So many consulting firms are themselves struggling to survive. They have got their own organisational problems–HR/ manpower problems, knowledge problems, financial problems, infrastructure problems, relevant exposure problems etc. So many companies are struggling to survive inspite of so many consultants being available in the market.

Corporate corruption, which is one of the main causes of organizational dysfunction, has not been addressed by the management consultants. Their reluctant thrust in this sphere has naturally been passive, stressing only on procedures rather than on apprehending and driving away the corrupt. Coercive methods or procedural changes can achieve limited results which has been proved in reality. If we really want to cure the root cause then the corporate character has to to be transformed.

Many consulting firms/audit firms were involved in corruption or manipulation which had already come to light. A recent example, as a per newspaper report, KPMG will pay $22 million-the largest payout ever by an accounting firm in a U.S. Securities and Exchange Commission action-to settle charges involving its audits of Xerox Corporation from 1997 through 2000, the SEC said on 19.04.05. KPMG allowed office documents group Xerox to manipulate its accounting during those years to close a $3 billion "gap" between actual operating results and results reported to the public, the SEC said.

The accounting firm permitted Xerox to inflate revenues by $3 billion and profit by $1.5 billion during the period, by accelerating revenue bookings on long term Xerox copier leases and by manipulating" cookie jar" reserves, the SEC said. KPMG agreed to pay a civil penalty of $10 million, to pay back the $9.8 million in audit fees it earned from Xerox during the years in question, and to pay additional prejudgement interest.

Can any doctor ensure any individual's sound health unless the person is genuinely interested? Food, medicine, doctors, medical books/knowledge are available in the market but at the end of the day, the individul's mind should be sincerely interested in ensuring the quality of his health. Some people rightly believe that "Consultant is somebody who borrows your watch to tell you the time. And, also sends you a bill for the service". Consultants and management gurus are making big bucks by selling trendy theories and jargons to unsuspecting advice seekers who consider their opinions as gospel truth and do not have the thinking ability to challenge the consultant's ideas.

If a consultant can study the market properly, predict the future growth of the industry, socio-economic development trends, map the political scenario, competitors strategy and the technological development so accurately why then they themselves do not start a company? Consultants are like astrologers, who will predict now, things that will happen in future. They may not be available there. They do not have any stake. They will conveniently find out a theory to justify the failure also. Jack Trout as quoted in *The Times of India*: "what is unfortunate is that so many great companies have followed the advice of consultants and now find themselves on the brink of disaster. And that's because too many consultants will tell clients exactly what they want to hear, instead of being objective advisers who look you in the eye and give you the good news with the bad."

In final analysis, a consultant cannot make a socio-economic value creating institution since for transforming the mind-core values, passion, creativity, determination and commitment are required which no consultant can provide.

Consultants cannot inspire creativity, research innovation. Enthusiasm cannot be purchased or taken on loan. If organisations really want to build a long term competitive advantage, they must be perceived by customers and society as fair, transparent, ethical and trustworthy.

Corporate Social Responsibility is a Hypocrisy

Milton Friedman once stated: "Business of business is business." Hence, many experts argued that the corporate community should not have any responsibility beyond shareholders' value. This is a great trap and excuse. Corporate community will bargain for all sorts of advantages from the society and the government; even companies are trying hard to keep the interest rate low so that cheap capital is available and all sorts of concessions are given by the governemnt, along with all sorts of protection. But do not talk about society or social resposibility, that is not their business. They are ready to spend crores of rupees for PR exercise, junk advertisements, manipulating the government policies, throwing extravagant parties and maintaining lavish lifestyles but seem not at all interested for contribution to society and social good.

Corporate social responsibility should not be confused with charity or philanthropy. Organisations must have genuine concern for value creation keeping in mind the society, economy and environment. Socio-economic value creation should be incorporated in the business model.

We are trying to invent a new concept like ROC, social marketing etc. But unless we change the basic premise nothing will work. Business of business is to create socio-economic value: this should be the basic premise.

If organisations are really interested for 'social responsibility', they have to ensure at least following responsibilites as suggested by Swaraj Paul in an article 'Wealth and Responsibility.'

- To obey the law.
- To serve society.
- To be fair to those one deals with(employees, customers, suppliers etc.)
- To protect investors.
- To encourage moral values.

In reality how many companies have accepted these responsibilities and how many are truly practising these? Unfortunately very few.

Swaraj Paul also advised that the responsibilities of wealth are the most difficult to accept, yet the most needed, in the areas of self-restraint. Wealth imparts arrogance, and arrogance combined with power of wealth can become a social menace. This is both a moral necessity and a practical protection. Wealth without responsibility, the attitude of the greedy in a needy world,provokes the reaction that causes the loss of wealth.

As per him only moral values can ensure responsibility. This basically means that the Corporate character is the compass or the key driving force for ensuring social good as rightly suggested by Anant G Nadkarni, GM, Group Corporate Social Responsibility, Tata Council for Community Initiatives in an article:" Today, there is a need to become responsible, truthful and efficient in all the many little things we do and become really useful as we serve others and ourselves."

Corporate Governanace is a Myth

Corporate governance codes have been introduced since the Cadbury Code on Best Practice was adopted by the UK twelve years ago. And this has been more the case in the last few years when one accounting scandal after another revealed the brazenness by which corporate management had violated the letter and spirit of financial and legal regulations, and blurred the thin dividing line between the bending of rules and breaking them.

Separate codes have been developed in other countries and in India, too, improvement of corporate governance has become a priority. The codes vary in scope and detail from country to country but their underlying objectives are essentially the same:

- To influence the institutions that govern the management-shareholder relationship so that one, and all shareholders are treated fairly.
- Management is motivated to maximise operational efficiency.
- Insider power is not abused and corporate resources are not squandered.
- The interests of the minority shareholder and society are safeguarded.

But how many companies are honestly interested to follow the above basics of governance? Enron, Worldcom, AOL, Tyco, GTB, UTI scam and several others published and unpublished scandals are great examples that corporate governance is nothing but lip service. Bishwajit Bhattacharyya, in a recent article commented: "That raises the question of corporate governance in India. Presently it is nothing but institutionalised misgovernance....companies should be managed by a board and not by the whims, personal aspirations and political affiliations of individual promoters. We have to move from the era of individual misgovernance to corporate governance."

Some of the companies are observing a 'Vigilance Awareness Week' to stop corruption. But in reality this is nothing but eye wash. As per various reports the companies which are observing Vigilance Weeks are the most corrupted. Transperancy, openness and accountability in systems alone can ensure that companies stand the test of vagaries of time.

Corporate governance should ensure transparency,fairness and accountability to all stakeholders. It is a prerequisite for integrity and credibility of the market and participating institutions. The confidence and trust in the efficacy of a corporate allows its access to the market, domestic and overseas, and helps it to make credible commitments to creditors, employees and others.

Corporate governance is not just a matter of prescribing a particular corporate structure and complying with a number of rules or standards. There is a need for broad principles. All concerned should then apply these flexibly and with common sense to the varying circumstances of individual enterprises. Ethical behaviour is not an output of codes of ethics or codes of conduct, it's a human activity shaped on a daily basis by the existing organisational and social structure.

Robert Monks and Nell Minow wrote in their book,*'Power and Accountability*: "Corporations determine far more than any other institution the air we breathe,the quality of water we drink, even where we live.Yet they are not accountable to any one."

Despite the recent increases in government regulations, corporate governance parameters, corporate ethics committees, auditors or consultants' review or audit of the companies, opinion polls suggest that confidence of the civic community in business and business community is at all time low. Corporate governance has become a formality. L.C.Gupta, a former member of Sebi rightly observed an: "It is well recognised that corporate governance goes far beyond legal technicalities and niceties. It involves ethical and social issues, not always easily defined because of constant change. Of course, legal compliance is a must but that is not enough from the governance angle."

Only corporate character can ensure mangement discipline or good conduct in respect of quality of product/ services, protection of investors interest, social responsibility, accountability, and integrity of all business activities.

Unless organisations sincerely accept that 'corporate credibility' is a core value and social trust is a critical asset for survival and growth, nothing will work. Corporate character has to be liberated and transformed otherwise it cannot control the behaviour of the few as described by Edith Wharton in her classic *'The House of Mirth'*: "A handful of vulgar people, bent only on spending and enjoying, may seem a negligible factor in the social development of the race; but they become an engine of destruction through the illusions they kill and the generous ardours they turn to despair. In what aspect could a society of irresponsible pleasure-seekers be said to have on the 'old woe of the world' any deeper bearing than the people composing such a society could guess? The answer is that a frivolous society can acquire a dramatic significance only through what its frivolous destroy. Its tragic implication lies in its power of debasing people and ideals."

Good governance in the ultimate analysis depends on character. One ancient and one modern explanation will validate the importance of character:

"The earth is upheld by the veracity of those who have subdued their passion, and following righteous practices, are never contaminated by desire, covetousness, and wrath."-*Visnu Purana* 3.12

"With all the power that a president has,the most important thing to bear in mind is this: you must not give power to a man unless, above every thing else, he has character. Character is the most important qualification the President of the United states can have"-Richard Nixon.

CRM (Customer Relationship Management) is Irrelevant

Hype or hyperbole of CRM has already faded.Some people are jokingly telling CRM stands for 'Casual Response Management'. Some people are questioning the relevance of CRM. It has already become another fad and a wastage of money and effort. Some people already started suggesting that CRM should be replaced by ROC (Return On Customer) or CEM (Customer Experiential Management). We are totally confused. Certainly CRM is not working. There is big a question mark about its effectiveness.

Lior Arussy, Founder and President of the Strativity Group explained in a lucid manner the reasons for failure of CRM in an interview published in *The Indian Management*, (Nov, 04 issue which I think is one of the best reflections of ground realities: ".........All are failing in the same consistent way–they treat the customer in a transactional way and not in an emotional way. They do not have a holistic view. They do not design the complete experience. There is no end-to-end experience for the customer. The other thing that we are seeing happening is that when companies are successful they become complacent. After a period, competitive changes will force customer preference change. The competitive landscape changes, technology changes. In all, these companies are trying to maximise profit from the previous experience as opposed to coming up with new ideas and more value propositions."

Food/Health are Product Kills–Who Bothers?

Food is most critical for human existence.In India several million people are suffering from diabetes, blood pressure,heart diseases, hypertensions and several other diseases. The social and economic cost of these diseases are huge. As per studies ,one of the main contributing factors is food. The pertinent question is: whether the quality and content of the various foods, bevearages or habit forming products available in the market arecontributing for long term health and healthy practices? In most of the cases the answer is a big no. The big brands do not disclose nutrition facts till they are forced to by legislation. There is no comprehensive information system that gives accurate and clear food composition. Customers do not get accurate information in terms of nutrition value, salt content and other important ingredients.

Several MNCs are dumping their products in India. Several food products are junk in terms of quality and in effect on health. These products are marketed by creating pseudo-aspirations and impulses to purchase and consume. Every body knows that high carbohydrates, high fat and high salt foods are harmful for health but they are being marketed freely by creating artificial value by clever advertisement like potato chips.

As published in a newspaper: McDonald's Corp will pay $8.5 million to settle a law suit accusing the fast-food giant of failing to inform consumers of delays in a plan to reduce fat in the cooking oil used for its popular French Fries and other foods. BanTrans Fats.com, a non-profit advocacy group, sued McDonald's in a California state court in 2003, alleging the company did not effectively disclose to the public that it had not switched to a healthier cooking oil.

In September 2002, McDonald's announced it would lower transfat in its cooking oils and said the switch would be completed in five months. In February 2003, McDonald's announced a delay. The lawsuit accused the Oak Brook, Illinois-based conmpany of failing to adequately inform consumers of that delay. The agreement announced on 09.02.05 requires McDonald's to pay $7 million to the American Heart Association to use the proceeds to educate the public about trans fats in foods. Heart-clogging trans fat is made when manufacturers add hydrogen to vegetable oil-a process called hydrogenation. The settlement also requires McDonald's to spend $1.5 million publicising that it has not followed through on its 2002 pledge.

As per a newspaper report, the food industry has been mired in a controversy over allegation of pesticide content in food products. Recently, the Rajasthan High Court issued show-cause notices to 47 food companies, including Indian and multinational food and beverages firms, for not specifying pesticide content on product labels. The show-cause notices were issued following a petition stating that food materials, particularly packed products made by 47 food companies, have a pesticide content higher than the prescribed Maximum Residue Limit(MRL).

In most of the cases the companies are taking advantage of lack of information and knowledge about the long term impact or effects on our body and the resultant cost and suffering.Is any company really interested in our health? The use of highly saturated animal fats to fry potatoes,the use of substances like monosodium glutamate, highly sweetened acidic aerated beverages, artificially fattened meat and many other low quality and harmful foods, and beverages are regularly sold in the market place without bothering about the health of the consumers and social cost. Most of the companies are not at all bothered in providing information to consumers regarding-nutrition value,ingredients and any harmful effect on health. Most of the products are also marketed with the so-called creative advertising which ultimately go into forming bad health practices and habits among the people.

As per a newspaper report, food firms do not appreciate the new quality guidelines. If the food processing industry's reaction to the government's proposed law which will help pinpoint the various stages at which contaminants are introduced into food items is anything to go by, consumers counts for nothing. The government has been forced to act to clean up the food processing mess following the SUDAN I fiasco in which 470 products which contain the suspected carcinogen have been recalled in 15 nations at a cost of several million dollars. Given the condition of Indian food processing sector it is virtually impossible to trace at which stage of production, processing or packaging the contaminant entered.

Processed food and beverage companies have been arguing about how listing ingredients and contaminants such as pesticides on labels would have a negative impact on their sales. They want a free hand to peddle toxic substances and not even give the consumer the choice of rejecting their products. The government's plan is in keeping with the internatuional laws like 2002 EU, one which makes it mandatory to trace their journey of food from production to processing to packaging. Is anybody really bothering about the presence of pesticides in colas and mineral water, heavy metals in condiments and detergents in milk and milk products?

Several medicines which are having harmful side-effects and banned in other countries still being marketed in India. We know the story of 'thalidomide'. As per a recent newspaper report an ingredient in certain cough and cold pills called Phenyl Propanolamine(PPA) can cause a stroke. But still doctors prescribe these drugs–sold over the counter as popular brands–despite alternatives being available. As per a report, India's pharma industry has over 1,00,000 formulations, many of which are 'irrational' in therapeutic terms. The government has failed to come up with a cohesive essential drugs list, on the lines of that prepared by WHO which names just 250 generics. Pharma industry also did not take any genuine initiative to bench-mark the generics in line with the list prepared by WHO.

On 30 September 2004, American drug major Merck pulled its $2.5 billion-a-year painkiller rofecoxib, branded Vioxx, off world markets. The reason: a higher risk of heart attack and stroke in patients who had taken it for more than 18 months. The drug had been in the market for six years,and had been prescribed more than 100 million times in the US alone. The recall, billed the largest in the industry's history, unleashed a slew of consumer law suits against Merck. It also turned the spotlight sharply on drug safety, and not just in the US.

In India, media reports pointed out that rofecoxib had a market worth over Rs.100 crore, with brands from industry heavyweights like Ranbaxy, Dr. Reddy's Labs, Lupin and Unichem. Drugs Controller General of India(DCGI) was quick to call a meeting of National Pharmacovigilance Advisory Committee(NPAC). The committee comprised experts from the medical community, academia and the government. Vioxx or copies of it made by Indian pharma companies were withdrawn on the recommendation of NPAC. NPAC did the correct thing. But for most part, consumer action groups and even doctors maintain that India's capacity to protect people from life -threatening side effects caused by medicines remains extremely inadequate. For instance, if Merck had not withdrawn Vioxx, it would have still been widely sold in India. More importantly, NPAC's advice is based on Merck's actions, and not on India-specific data.

No doubt, the Vioxx case put the American drug regulator on the backfoot. But in India, it has exposed the inadequacy of the system to spot trends in adverse drug reactions(ADRs)–jargon for side effects–in the Indian population after a drug hits the market. Still, in India, there is no proper reporting or recording system for adverse drug reactions. Who cares about the health of the people?

Doubt in Baby Products

If a newspaper report is to be believed, there is serious doubt about the quality of even baby products. The Food and Drug Administration, Maharashtra, recently, has issued a showcause notice to Johnson & Johnson for 'mis-branding' its baby products,especially its baby oil. The agency has alleged that these products do not carry the necessary "clinical properties or specifications" for children. The FDA said that it had acted on a complaint from a consumer.

Commissioner A.Ramakrishnan noted that the label on the baby oil bottle declared the "key ingredients" in terms of their vitamin content but did not mention the base-99.9% light liquid paraffin. "This oil shouldn't exclusively be marketed as baby oil because liquid praffin is not recommended for use of infants", he said. The ingredients mentioned on the packaging are 'Vitamin D3, Vitamin A Palmitate,Vitamin E acetate'.

The notice issued by FDA covered almost the entire range of Johnson & Johnson's baby products including baby oil, baby hair oil, lotion, and baby shampoo. "There have been no clinical trials to brand the product a special baby product. The company has no permission from the Drug Controller General of India for the same. In this situation the product fails to qualify as a baby product," said Ramakrishnan.

The company's baby products "do not figure in the BIS list of approved cosmetic products for specific use by children and infants," the FDA notice says.

Johnson's Baby Oil is a leading product in the babycare segment of its business. The babycare market is estimated to be worth over Rs.200 crore. Johnson & Johnson dominates the market, with a share of almost 75%.

Environment Quality-Who Cares?

India is still at the bottom of the class in conserving natural resources and providing clean drinking water. A new environment sustainability index ranks India as one of the worst polluters, rating it 101 of 146 countries when assessed on parameters like air pollution, biodiversity and water quality.'

How green is your country' index, was produced by a team of environmental experts at Yale and Columbia universities and released at the World Economic Forum in Davos in January 2004, on which countries were ranked on 21 elements of environmental sustainability. It has a holistic list which factored in not only environmental pollution and health but also government management efforts,contribution to protection of global natural resources,and a country's capacity to meet environmental challenges overtime. India's performance has improved from 2002 when it ranked 116 in the environment sustainability index. But it is still pathetic and below average in environmental quality parameters: air pollution, and efforts to reduce it, biodiversity, land degradation, water quality and adequate supply and greenhouse emissions.

Money is Honey–Main Mantra

Black or white, money is honey. A section of the society's fundamental premise being: don't bother about the colour of money, just enjoy the power of money. At present, black money is estimated to be about 40% of the GDP. Various agencies and individuals have tried to assess the total volume of unaccounted cash in the system and have arrived at different figures. In 1985, the National Institute of Public Finance and Planning (NIPFP) estimated the size of black economy at 20% of legitimate economy for 1980-81. Later, economist S B Gupta reckoned the black economy to be worth 42% of GDP for 1980-81 and 51% for 1987-88. JNU Professor Arun Kumar estimated the cash economy in 1995 at 40% of GDP. As per Kumar the estimate holds true today. So, every year, India generates black money worth Rs.11.50 lakh crores.

Most of this unaccounted money goes out of the country or is stored as gold. As per one estimate, so far, Indians have stashed away $150 billion overseas. Many businessmen strip corporate assets, drive companies to bankruptcy and divert funds overseas. A lot of money which has been taken out of the country comes back as foreign investment or foreign institutional investment. In 2004, around $18 billion came via FIIs and FDI investment, some of which was recycled black money.

As per expert, if the entire black money is converted into white, India's growth would get boosted to 10%, all educated youth would get jobs. The additional tax collection of about Rs.3 lakh crore would leave a fiscal surplus.

Unless 'character' is changed the 'colour' of money will remain irrelevant. It will be a mere illusion to change black money into white money. Professor Arun Kumar who has written a book on the subject rightly observed: "Black money is not only an economic phenomenon:it has political, social and historical dimensions too. The main reason for its generation is the unholy nexus between politicians and bureaucrats, on the one hand, and businessmen on the other; one helps the other in fuelling the black economy."

Huge Inventory of Cash–Is it Efficiency?

A recent newspaper report: As per one study of the balance sheet of 1000 companies for 2004-05,100 companies are having cash/liquid asset of Rs1000 crore each. Mostly, these liquid assets are in the form of bank deposits, cash in hand, debentures/bonds, government securities and mutual funds. As per the study as reported in the news paper,about Rs.1,00,000 crore are lying in banks and liquid assets. The study did not include banks and financial companies. As per the study about Rs 50000/- crore lying only in bank deposits. Several big and famous companies are also in the list.

Companies are trying to justify the excess inventory of cash/cash flow due to:

- Improved sales
- Improved productivity/profitability
- Delay in capital expenditure decision

The pertinent question is what is the opportunity cost of this near dead cash or assets. Whose money is being underutilised? Who is accountable for the proper capital allocation model to utilise the scarce resources?

By itself money is no use. It is dead asset. It has to be productively and timely utilised to get maximum value addition which will have multiplier effect in the economy. If the surplus cash is invested,employment and income will be generated in the economy and as a result demand for various goods and services also will be increased.

Corporate sector continuously lobbying with the government for free access to FDI whereas this piece of study clearly revealed that corporate sector not at all efficient to utilise even their internally generated surplus or capital for further growth development of the company as well as the economy.

If companies cannot prepare efficient capital allocation model–who is to blame. What is the relevance of so-called talented CEOs and business leaders who can't take timely decision to properly utilise surplus funds. Huge amount of money is being kept as cash/liquid assets and merrily companies are accepting even net negative return if inflation is factored in for adjustment. We are actually fooling ourselves at the cost of huge national loss since this money belongs only to the public.

Corporate sector should revisit the 'corporate finance' and prepare the capital/resource allocation model in the best interest of the company and the country. Urgent sincere initiative in this direction is required.

Corporate sector should realise: this is ultimately public money and they have the moral and professional responsibility to ensure its effective utilisation. They should not suffer from 'satisfactor underperformance' syndrome.

The importance of 'Present value of money' and 'potential value of money' should be understood in real sense. Keeping money idle or underutilised is the reflection of gross ineffciency and mis-management in every sense of economic and social parameters and cannot be justified by any excuse.

Vanishing Companies: Visible Victims

As per a newspaper report, out of the 229 companies initially identified as "vanishing", the latest figure released by the Minister of State of Company Affairs is around 92 while the remaining companies reportedly have resurfaced. Vanishing companies owe to the public about Rs.800 crore, while the resurfaced companies are accountable for over Rs 900 crore.

Prosecution has so far been launched under the Companies Act 1956 and FIRs have been filed under the Indian Penal Code against the directors and promoters of 76 vanishing companies. According to the Minister of State for Company Affairs, several steps, including greater co-operation with various state governments and keeping a watch on the antecedents of various companies have also been taken. Sebi has debarred 100 companies and 378 directors of vanishing companies from associating with the capital market for five years. Sebi has also issued notices to 22 merchant bankers who handled public issues of 15 vanishing companies.

Nobody knows how long it will take to recover money from these companies and reimburse to the investors or the victims.Who knows, whether the promoters,directors, merchant bankers and auditors of all these companies will be finally held responsible and punished.

Company Board is a Rubber Stamp

As per the corporate governance guidelines board should play an effective and effecient role to guide, control and check the power of the CEO or Chairman so that the interest of the shareholders and customers are properly protected and the company is run in effective manner and not used as the private property of the CEO or Chairman.

Most directors of the board typically have similar age, education profiles, and possibly even belong to the same social and cultural network. This tends to get perpetuated because these group members look to induct people like themselves as new members. In order to avoid opposition and dissensions, 'trusted' people are inducted in the board. It has been observed that many board members do not have the requisite competence to understand the complexities of a particular business and to contribute meaningfully. There are board members who do not have the time and energy to concentrate and play any role in the governance of the company. Eventually they become the 'yes' man and only enjoy facilities and previleges. The ground reality thus being:

- Friends and family members are appointed who will only decorate the board.
- Independent directors are appointed who do not have much idea or understanding of the industry so that they cannot ask uncomfortable questions.
- Size of the board is kept deliberately small and efforts to appoint only 'own people.'
- Substantive issues/important policy matters are not always discussed in the board meetings.
- Agenda of the board meeting is circulated at the eleventh hour so that members can not do the home work properly.
- Ultimately CEO/Chairman becomes the source and distributor of power, knowledge and information and the board becomes passive or functions like a rubber stamp.

- In most of the cases the CEO/Chairman is sourrounded by *'chamchas, chelas and cronies.'*

No company can become an institution unless the board has a character: independent, trustworthy, transparent, efficient and effective. This is not easy to create. Unless the board is comprised of truly independent directors-this can not be ensured. An independent board can ensure that CEOs must perform or quit. Power is not concentrated in the hands of the CEO, but is shared among the members of the board to ensure good corporate governance and outstanding performance.

L.C. Gupta, former member of Sebi, who has been on many boards and seen them from inside explained the reality in a recent article: "......Most of our private-sector corporate boards still continue to be a chummy type of cozy clubs, lacking a questioning attitude. This kind of culture must go in order to improve the quality of deliberations and decision–making in the boards....."

Limited Companies Unlimited Distrust

When we talk about responsibility and accountablity, companies and their promoters or CEO s refer to company laws and acts to justify their responsibility to be limited towards shareholders only. But, when it comes to freedom and authority they want unlimited access to the country's resources, capital market, government sops, and unlimited power to make decisions and manipulate the customers. They are free do anything even at the cost of society but no body should raise any issue or create noise since they are creating wealth for the country by taking so much risk. Is it not balatant hypocrisy?

There are innumberable instances of criminal corporate negligence or corporate deceit-in the stock market, financial market, plundering and siphoning of public money, selling shoddy products, pocketing huge margin,evading taxes, manipulating information and even creating environmental disasters. Few examples are given.

One of the greatest examples of corporate deceit is the Bhopal gas tragedy. Twenty years ago, Bhopal choked over methyl isocynate fumes from the Union Carbide India Limited plant. According to The Madhya Pradesh Gas Relief and Rehabilitation Department, over 15000 lost their lives and 550,000 suffered serious injuries. Former UCC chief Warren Anderson, charged for culpable homicide, remains an absconder from Bhopal courts for a decade. Over 5.5 lakh individuals have on an average received Rs 25000 and the latest court order would entitle each person another Rs.25000. Is Rs 50,000 per person a compensation, or a pittance, for a people economically and physically destroyed over two generations? In 2001, Dow Chemicals acquired United Carbide Corporation, USA and said it owed nothing to the Bhopal gas victims. Dow claims that the 1989 settlement ruled by the Supreme Court had resolved all civil and criminal liabilities related to the disaster. Why will society trust corporate community? Is it not an unlimited deceit?

Another example of unlimited distrust is the cobweb ownership structure of most of promoter controlled companies. As per a newspaper report, several companies' main controlling shareholding (ownership) is too complex, like a cobweb. The shareholding is complicated to such an extent that some companies are controlled through hundreds of companies. Again these companies are controlled by other various layers of companies. The identity of these companies are not publicly known. There is a web of transactions among these entities.It will require great investigative skills and knowledge of corporate finance and taxation to find out who actually are the owner(s) of these companies and what is their source of funds.

In India, promoters control their companies mostly through investment companies and trusts. Investment companies are those entities which have been set up or function as companies that invest or have holdings in other companies, which raise funds and then buy and sell shares in other companies. Investment companies can also be holding companies. Here the idea is not to move in and out of companies for making a quick profit but rather to set in place a structure that facilitates the required level of holding in a particular company. Analysts say that these can be either used to mask the way a company is controlled by a promoter or to save on taxes. Also besides holding shares in the flagship company,these companies trade in them. Though this is not illegal, but this gives promoters a lot of scope for stock manipulation.

It will require great investigative skills and knowledge of finance and taxation to find out who actually the owner(s) of these companies are and the source of funds since most of the companies are private limited companies and exact details,either of the shareholding or the performance are often not easily available. Why is this holding pattern so complex? Is this the example of transparency or integrity? How can we expect society will trust the corporate community?

The present system of quarterly compliance reports submitted by companies to stock exchanges under clause 49 of the Listing Agreement would never be able to uncover many serious types of irregularities. It is a merely boxticking exercise. These quarterly reports mean a huge amount of paperwork but very little effect.

Example of how finances are being manipulated blatantly are : As per a newspaper report, US regulators filed civil fraud charges against former Qwest chairman and CEO Joseph Nacchio and eight others, alleging a scheme to vastly inflate the finances of the telecom giant. The Securities and Exchange Commission said it filed civil actions against the executives alleging that between 1999 and 2002, they" engaged in a multi-faceted fraudelent scheme designed to mislead the investing public about the company's revenue and growth". As a result of that scheme, Qwest "fraudulently recognised over $3 billion of revenue and excluded $71.3 million in expenses, "the SEC said in a statement. "Joseph Nacchio and others at Qwest wanted the company's shareholders to believe that the company was doing better than it actually was," said SEC Enforcement Direcor Stephen Cutler. "Today's enforcement action once again tells corporate executives that they will be held personally accountable when they keep the truth from the marketplace."

Qwest, the big regional telecom giant, settled its role in the case last year by agreeing to pay a $250 million penalty. "The disclosure fraud at Qwest was orchestrated at the highest level of the company to deceive investors", said Randall Fons, SEC Regional Director in Denver, Colorado.

"Qwest's CEO and other top executives projected revenue and earnings that they knew were overly aggressive, and then all of the defendants used smoke and mirrors to meet those unrealistic projections.These individuals must now answer for their conduct and the enormous decline in share holder value that they caused".

Example of how information is being manipulated are thus: Philip Morris, a top cigarette manufacturuer paid for and influenced scientific articles that discredited the link between passive smoking and sudden infant death, according to a new study on a once-secret industry document. The new study, prepared by researchers at the University of California, San Francisco and the US centres for Disease Control and Prevention, was published in the March issue of the journal *Pediatrics*, says Xinhua.

"Undermining people's understanding of the link between passive smoking and Sudden Infant Death Syndrome(SIDS) places infants everywhere at increased risk," said Stanton

Glantz, Director of the Centre for Tobacco Control Research and Education, and who is also a senior author of a new study analysing the tobacco company documents.

Analysis of the Philip Morris documents showed that the company sought and paid an author to write an article that was published in 2001 in a scientific journal. The firm guided his writing and suggested changes in his conclusions in order to call into question the published studies that show links between second-hand cigarette smoke and SIDS, the new report said. The article was cited in 19 other scientific papers, misleading physicians, their patients and researchers about the risk of exposure to passive smoking.

The study also showed that Philip Morris had budgeted $50,000-100,000 for hiring a scientist to write the paper they wanted and it continues to use this strategy to sow confusion about the real dangers of passive smoking and to distort the entire scientific process.

Another example of blatant hypocrisy: "I regret what happened and am ashamed that I did not take responsibility earlier,even though I was in charge of overseeing Daewoo's businesses", Kim Woo-Choong said in a written apology.

Kim Woo-Choong, former Chairman of Daewoo's group, who fled South Korea when it collapsed in 1999 with about $ 70 billion dollar in debt was arrested as he returned home on 14.06.05.

Kim Woo-Choong was once revered as the man who built Daewoo into one of the country's most powerful Chaebol or family-owned conglomerates who is now accused of having falsified Daewoo's accounts to draw billions of dollars to illegal bank loans before diverting them overseas.

Thousands of employees lost jobs, livelihood, hope and dignity. What is the use of apology?

2

Value Creation Debate & Confusion

The most urgent issue is the search for a new organisational architecture. Food education, environment, war and even love are subsidiary to this. Our organisations are anachronistic, our school are hopelessly flawed. Without a new design, the intermediate future will be as ungratifying (for the vast majority) as the times we live in.:-

Richardo Sember, Chairman, Semco group.

Today, it is not enough to manage effeciently and produce results. Values and means by which are done, are as important.—

Arun Maira

Acknowledgement of Problem / Crisis

Nothing is perfect in this world. Nothing is absolute in this world. Nothing is constant. Every thing is relative. Every thing is in a process of change in continuum. It is not sufficient to know the world. Important thing is that it is to be changed. For bringing change in the right direction we must be honest enough to accept that there is problem or necessity of change as Rosabeth Moss Kanter rightly commented in a recent interview: "......So the difference between winners and losers is not whether you have problems or troubles; it is whether you have the confidence to acknowledge them and fix them. "Any change ultimately depends on intention and purpose. In the previous chapter we have observed that the corporate sector is really in crisis:

- Crisis of social trust
- Crisis of growth and bottom line
- Crisis of theories
- Crisis of superficiality
- Crisis of corruption
- Crisis of acceptance of problem

In recent times, we have seen enough scandals about the corporations and CEOs-like Enron,Worldcom, AOL, Tyco. In India GTB,UTI, Home Trade Ltd. just to mention a few classic examples. If we are honest enough to solve the problem then we must first understand accept the problem. There is a crisis of corporate character due to the following:

- Unhealthy relationship
- Lack of transparency
- Lack of core values
- Injustice
- Dishonesty
- Both physical or and mental corruption
- Lack of social concern
- Excessive greed

We should sincerely believe that the 'Truth can be buried,but it cannot be killed. Truth has a way of rising from the grave and haunting the very people who conspired to bury it. ' We should be sincere to understand 'value creation' in real sense.

Value Equation / Perception

Let us understand what is the prevalent perception of the meaning of 'value creation'.

Presently the main perceptions are:

- Focus on utility value of product/services.
- Psychological value of product/ervices : glamour, aspirations, status symbol, uniqueness and all these are built through high cost brand building exercise.
- Benefit and cost
- Affordable price for an acceptable quality
- Optimum features-features actually required by customers at affordable price
- Low cost options or choices
- Stimulating customer experience
- Customer delight-delight in price,product/services and delight in experience.

Superficiality in Value Creation

There is an element of superficiality in the whole approach to creating value. The value creation concept presently practised is basically based around the following approach:

1. Target-customer centric
2. Competitor centric.
3. Profit/ROI centric.
4. Resource/capital centric.
5. Technology centric.

1. Given the incomplete data information, very few people are in a position to understand the true value of product or services. In most of the cases customers do not have any idea about the cost structure of the product or

services. In most of the cases customers do not have much idea about the intricaies of technology and also the real quality of the product. So called brand management, advertisement and promotion are used by companies to generate artificial differentiation without much real value creation. Sometimes companies take advantage due to lack of choice and options available to the customers.

2. Companies offer price product quality depending on the competition. There is no genuine concern for the customers.
3. Value creation model is decided on the basis of expected ROI not on the basis of customers' concern or social concern.
4. Value is created depending on the resource/capital availability—not because of customers' concern.
5. Value will be created as per choice of technology or availability of technology which again depends on the capital, competition, knowledge etc.

This superficial approach has to be changed. Corporate sector has to be honest about motives, means and ends. We should be really honest in the pursuit of social good or socio-economic value creation by understanding the customer, society and economic issues.

Money Nexus vs Value Nexus

Development with a human face or human centric development cannot be ensured by 'profit-money-share price' concept or mindset. This nexus cannot ensure social good/ value creation. Social goods basically depend on:

- Employment
- Empowerment through freedom of choice, access to knowledge & information.

- Equity-distributive justice-economic, political & cultural power to a vast majority of people.
- Ethical practices
- Ecology/environmental concern

'Profit-money-share price' equation will not be able to ensure effectiveness of the organisation in the 21st century market place. Social knowledge / average social consciousness is changing very fast due to dissemination of real time information knowledge. All constituents of the society-women, children, youth, adults, old are exposed to real time issues and are becoming more demanding day-by-day you cannot take the advantage of ignorance of the masses for long.

Today, the knowledge and information are to be used and synthesised creatively innovatively so as to produce goods and services with social insights. In order to achieve that 'profit-money-share price model' has to be replaced by a 'knowledge-creativity-innovation-socio-economic value creation model.'

Socio-Economic Value Matrix

By itself product services do not have any value unless they are required and purchased by the customers. Fundamental to survival of any product and service, and consequently the organisation, is to increase the market share and create new markets.

Organisation has to appreciate and study the socio-economic reality of the customers. Value is created in product services through physical and mental labour of human beings. Mental labour is a prime driving force for value creation. Through continuous creativity & innovation socio-economic value creation is possible. It is not a one-time affair. It is a continuous process. For this, creative interaction and connectivity with the socio-economic realities is very important, essantially to understand the opprtunity for innovation and value creation. Following are the fundamental aspects of soco-economic value matrix:

1. *Supply Side:*

To appreciate understand that a vast majority of people have low real per capita income and their purchasing power is very crucial. They have to be brought to the market place by providing 'choices' through relevant product /services with acceptable quality at lesser prices. Corporation's inefficiency, wastage, greed should not be factored in 'Pricing'. Recent example is ' mobile tariff' which was used to be about Rs.16 a minute when it all began and now has been reduced to less than Rs.1.00 per minute.

There are several areas where the vast majority of people's 'lifestyle' can be improved by introducing new products / services. To achieve that the corporation has to invest in innovation and creativity. If we really want to maximise the value equation we have to offer product and services keeping in mind the life style, convenience and purchasing power of the vast majority of 'disguised customers'. Companies have to understand some basic socio-economic data:

The estimated number of households in India is likely to be around 200 million by 2006-07. Out of this, about 82 million households would have annual income of Rs. 22000-45000. This is about 40% of the estimated numbers. Another 75 million households would be in the annual income range of Rs. 45000-215000, that is 38% of the projected households. Another 22% of the population would be having income below Rs. 22000 per annum.

Today, agriculture accounts for 24 percent of GDP, while Industry and services account for 25 percent and 51 percent respectively. About 57% of the work force is employed in agriculture, 18% in Industry and 25% in service sector respectively. Although poverty declined from 40 percent in 1990s to about 26 percent in 1999-2000, we still have 260 million people living below poverty line.

Unless you understand the ground reality, Products or Services cannot be offered with socio-economic insight or socio-economic solutions. Poor people should not be excluded from the so-called 'Market Segmentation' theory of the corporations.They should be considered potential customers. If we consider them as potential customers, the following automatically follow:

- Creativity/innovation will be directed towards new products / services development
- Market will expand—more number of people will come under the market system
- Economy of scale will be achieved
- Increase in purchasing power of people will increase
- There will be Increase in productivity level income level
- May decrease social distrust

Supply push basically means that continuous innovation is required to offer various products / services with socio-economic solutions and the solutions should cater to:

- Old people
- Women
- Children
- Urban/rural population
- Purchasing power centric
- Knowledge improvement centric

Dr. K. Sankaran, a professor at TAMPI rightly wrote:" ..Supply side competition is something our society has not thought through adequately. That free market economics is predicted upon supply side (i.e. the give side) is something we need to mull over and understand...The idea of marketing is rooted in the idea of keenly finding out what the consumer wants and giving choice to the customers,essentially on the give side."

Also focus on supply side can ensure real choice to the customers and the real choice has significant economic, social, cultural and political implications. Observations made by Rajiv Desai in a recent editorial of the *Times Of India* is quite relevant: "The privilegentsia is an outgrowth of the state-centric model of governance that India pursued for most of its life as an independent country. It refers to the clutch of bureaucrats, politicians and academicians who ruled over the fate of millions of decent, hardworking people ...Influence peddling and kickbacks were part for the course in the India of old. Either you paid extra cash or used influence. The ability to get things done without black payment was a mark of a person's social status.......The explosion of choice has challenged both the black market and the privilengentsia raj."

Corelation between Price and Intrinsic value

There should be a correlation between 'price'of products/ services and the 'intrinsic value'offered to the customers. The gap has to be continuously minimized. The inefficiency, wasteful expenditure and non-improvement approach should not be covered up in 'pricing system' to exploit the customers. It has been observed in many products / services,when competition comes immediately the pricing strategy is changed and overnight Rs.70 / kg reduced to Rs.50 / kg or within a few months Rs.16 /minute becomes Rs.1 / minute without any fundamental change in the economic cost structure. This is simply cheating the customers. Several so-called excellent companies played the high margin game to cover up their huge overhead costs, and lack of product innovation taking advantage of customers' uninformed perception and lack of choices available in the market place.

Things have already started changing due to the emergence of a new breed of low cost manufacturers who are providing acceptable quality at a much less cost. Days are gone for the unreasonable gap between price and intrinsic value of product and services.

Most developed and developing countries' economies are mainly driven by consumer spending. High quality,low price and prompt delivery have enabled Chinese goods manufacturers to flood the world's markets with their products. They provide value for their customers' money which leads to brand equity and loyality. This is the right approach for value creation. There is no point in wasting crores of rupees on useless, junk advertisements which only create temporary hype without much significance in reality. Another example was shown by Wal-Mart by offering high quality goods at prices 30-40% cheaper than its competitors.

Through continuous innovation in product design, in operations, logistics,procurement and distribution value is to be created in a real sense. Mere customer focus and lip service to CRM/CVM will not help at all in the long run.

Quality and service mindset

Excellent quality has to be ingrained in the organisation's mind-set. Quality of product / service should be an integral part of the business model. Organisation should sincerely believe that 'there is no finish line' in quality/service.' Without top management's commitment excellent quality of product/ service can not be achieved.

Excellent quality/service is not a matter of mere procedure, it should be approached in a scientific way. To achieve high quality or high service organisation one must approach it in a scientific manner by precisely defining what is meant by excellent quality / service, identifying what is important to the customer and accordingly measuring how well an organisation performs in meeting customer requirements and expectati ons. A consistent excellent quality of product or service is extremely difficult to achieve and requires a great deal of effort and commitment from the top management.

Most of the organisations make the mistake by assuming that they know what the customer wants and expects in terms of service and quality. Decisions are taken to achieve things that customers do not really care about while ignoring those what customers really want. This is because often the key-decision makers have a very low level of contact with the customers whereas customers' contact / interface with the lowest hierarchical level is more frequent. Knowing the needs of the customers in order of importance and translating and ensuring delivery system should form the fundamentals of quality strategy.

Organisations' attitude has to be aligned in that direction. Quality should not be considered as a ritual, it should become the habit of the organisation. "As Stephen Covey observed in his book" *Seven Habits of Highly Effective People*: "Excellence is not an act,it is a habit."

2. Demand side

Main issue is how to create employment or opportunities for income generation. Untapped talents of a vast majority of people and unused / under-used resources of the country can be utilised if continuous innovation and creativity is channelised in a commercially viable way and produce new products /services and a new way of engaging people in the value generation chain. One example is rural development / rural marketing. Still thousands of acres of land are barren or not utilised or under utilised. Rural population can be utilised for rural marketing and development by proper training. Cost of manpower also will be much cheaper.

Relevance of technology

We have to understand what makes customers adopt new technology. It has to make things easy for customers' life. Consumers are often very confused due to advertisements of various dimensions which are superficial in nature. People want simplicity. There are very few people who buy gadgets for the sake of buying. By and large most consumers will invest in technology if it makes their life productive,keeps them safe or makes them better informed. People will invest and adopt to technology if it is easy to use, affordable and makes their life better.

There must be a conviction that technology is the key for developing new products / services or benefits and in making them affordable. This requires careful investment in the right talent and in infrastructure. Technology per se is neutral. Technology with a human element only can create value. Bill Gates,Chairman, Microsoft said: "The first rule of any technology used in a business is that automation applied to an efficient operation will magnify the effeciency. The second is that automation applied to an inefficient operation will magnify the inefficiency."

There should be a convergence of technology and socio-economic value creation. This is possible if we consider people first, gadget /equipment / technology next. Technology will be relevant if it ensures the following:

- Cost-effectiveness or affordability
- Time effectiveness
- User-friendly-in making things easier and more productive

- Convenience
- Excitement and effeciency

If we consider people first, automatically focus will be on the people instead of product design / technology. Creativity and innovation will be guided by the people's requirement, and the market will automatically grow and new customers will enter in the market. How many people can afford to purchase 'Main Frame' computer though it is technologically well designed? Creativity / innovation in technology should be guided by the philosophy of 'People First'.

Technology will be useful and relevant if it reaches the common people. For instance, Shyam Telecom in Rajasthan opted to take its phones to the people rather than wait for them to come to it. The company has equipped a fleet of cycle rickshaws with mobile phones. Drivers pedal these mobile payphones throughout Jaipur and the surrounding countryside. Two hundred rickshaw drivers were largely drawn from those at the margins of society—the disabled and women. The drivers made a 20 percent margin on every call, earning between Rs.6000 and Rs 9,000 per month.

"In the 21st century real growth and prosperity will depend on how a business problem is meshed with technology. Technology is pushing itself to solve business problems and create better innovative applications, and that's where invention will occur."- says Nick Donofrio, Senior VP, IBM.

Gap between potential demand and actual demand

As per one estimate,on an average, of a 1000 households, only about 56 own a washing machine,122 own a colour TV, 280 a black and white TV, 120 a refrigerator,128 a mixer/ grinder and 308 a pressure cooker. About 44% of the households use toothpaste, another 36 percent tooth powder, 26 percent hair wash items and 58 percent utensil cleaners.

Recently the government announced the results of NSS (National Sample Survey) conducted by the National Sample Survey Organisation. Some important data pertaining to consumption/demand is as follows:

Item/product	Category	% of population who own
TV	Urban areas Rural areas	66 26
Fridge	Urban areas Rural areas	28 04
Phone/Cell	Urban areas Rural areas	26 06
PC	Urban areas Rural areas	1.4 0.67
Washing Machines	Urban areas Rural aeas	11 01

Another important data: about 29 percent of urban population are living on rent, 6 percent being provided house by employers which means that more than one third of the urban population did not have a house of their own.

There is a tremendous scope in unlocking the rural/semi-urban demand by offering affordable options and also engaging these people in various economic / business activities in rural or semi-urban areas.

Demand cannot be generated without employment.India has the largest youth population in the world. About 34 percent of India's population is less than 15 years old. Most of these 350 million young Indians will need jobs in the next few years. A sustained growth in GDP is essential to create jobs and the jobs have to be created in rural and semi-urban areas. Cities or urban areas are already overburdened. Rural population is required to be brought to the value creation system by innovative and creative business model. We should remember the essence of a Chinese proverb: "Give a man a fish, and he'll eat for a day. Teach him how to fish and he'll eat forever."

Consumption is a key driving force of economic development. More than one third of the Indian population is below poverty level. To reduce poverty levels, per capita income needs to be around $2000 per annum compared to the present $500. To achieve that huge opportunities for income generation are required. Majority of Indian population entering their prime consumption years, will be wasted unless income levels increase very fast.

3. Socio-Cultural side/social innovation

Contributions are to be made by the corporate sector in education, health, drinking water, sanitation, rural development and infrastructure development. Above all the corporate community should lead / motivate the civic society on how to create value through sharing of information, knowledge, innovation, creativity, managerial expertise and transform the 'average socio-economic mind or consciousness' of the people. Corporate community can contribute and influence all aspects of socio-cultural life of the civic community by guiding and inspiring them. It's a question of intention only.

Corporate leaders must have the human purpose. Corporate leaders should take initiative to blend technology, innovativeness and managerial expertise with social capacities to encourage the participation of a vast majority of population. Corporate leaders can influence to shape the 'social character 'as William C Miller rightly said: "People everywhere are starving for leadership ....starving to connect with leader who are believable, trustworthy, and capable of actualising constructive changes. We need leaders who can transform the character of the organisations and curtail the exploitation of people and natural resources, inequalities of educational and economic access, and stress from an impossible pursuit of happiness through unlimited desires and acquisitiveness."

The vast majority of people should be given access to opportunities and possibilities. To achieve that they should be encouraged and also product or services should be provided with socio-economic insights. A good example as given by C.K.Prahalad "Just translating the web into multiple languages is not enough. It still assumes that people who are using it are very literate. How do you get people who cannot read to participate? People don't think beyond just key words, yet data bases, websites and search engines are structured only that way. We need to go from just the ability to search for information to the creation of knowledge and in sight that people can act on."

Corporate sector can make a huge difference to people's health and reduce the social cost and suffering of the people by taking creative actions and introducing programmes to increase the awareness of people in food, health habits and also introducing various good quality food / health products to improve the health of the masses and transform the health habits.

If intention is there, social innovation / social good can become an integral part of business model... One excellent example is the Usha Martin group. The group operates one of the well managed NGOs in Ranchi called Krishi Gram Vikas Kendra(KGVK).

Started in 1972, KGVK aims at facilitating self-sustainability within the Ranchi community through various projects it undertakes under the Total Village Management Programme. At present, KGVK has a presence in 352 villages, assists 50,000 households, and has reached 345,000 individuals in Ranchi,

Saraikela, and Hazaribagh districts. It has 120 regular members on its pay roll and spends about Rs1 crore on administrative costs. One of the important projects undertaken by KGVK is the Integrated Watershed Development Project-which has taken up 20,000 hectares of watershed project in Gamaria, Rajnagar, Getalsud and Patratu, which will assist irrigation in the region, provide drinking water, improve health, facilitate education, and empower women.

Apart from the water project, KGVK runs two rural hospitals in Rukka and Narayan Soso, and 13 health sub-centres. The hospitals house 15 beds each and are equipped with ultra-sound facility, ECG, operation theatre, labour room, and pathology laboratory. Other health initiatives are child immunisation camps, family planning awareness, and village hygiene and sanitation programmes through its trained health workers.

KGVK has also set up 600 self-help groups that are involved in poultry, goatery, piggery, papad-making, mushroom growing, etc, 500 of them run by women. Because of this initiative women have started contributing to family income. All these initiatives have significantly contributed in bringing social transformation in those areas.

In India, the Amul-model is the best example of social innovation. The Amul model of co-operatives, backed by sophisticated processing technologies, ushered in the White Revolution, taking India to the top of the milk-producing countries even as it transformed the rural economy.

Another excellent example of social innovation / investment is the Grameen Bank movement in Bangladesh, a brainchild of Professor Muhammad Yunus. Grameen bank is now the largest NGO in the world. This has restored faith, dignity and hope among rural women using micro-credit. Grameen Bank in Bangladesh pioneered micro-credit societies consisting entirely of rural women, who traditionally had no property, spending power or credit worthiness. Grameen Bank proved that poor rural women could be relied on to repay loans with commercial interest and with hardly any default. Micro-loans were used first for improved consumption and then for starting female-owned businesses.

Grameen Bank inspired the mushrooming of similar outfits like BARC, which diversified micro-credit into schools with female teachers, greatly improving female literacy. Next came Grameen Telephones : rural women obtained mobiles on credit, and used these to operate rural public call offices. The main contributions of these initiatives were:

- Empowerment of rural women
- Spread of education/literacy
- Control of female fertility
- Unleashed women's potential for economic and social change.

Another example of social innovations is the initiative taken by Cemex, the world's 3rd largest company. Cemex resolved to tap the market of low income groups and succeeded remarkably. In 1998 it launched Patrimonio Hoy (PH or Property Today) as an experimental programme intended to enable poor people to pay for building materials and services that would upgrade their homes. PH customers were asked to form groups of three and take joint responsibility for making weekly payments. Their payments entitle them to a room's worth of quality building materials. The customers also become members of the local Patrimonio Hoy club, which gives them technical advice on designing their rooms, warehousing privileges, and other preferred customer rights with the local retailer.

With the Patrimonio Hoy offer, DIY(Do-It-Yourself) customers build at approximately three times the traditional rate and at a fourth-fifths of traditional cost and are often repeat customers. After three years of operation, Cemex had 39,000 families as members and over $10 m in extended credit.Importantly, the customer base is reportedly growing at over 1,500 every month, while the rate of payment is a staggering 99.6%.

The success of these initiatives of social innovations highlights the significance of leveraging social trust as collateral in the low and marginalised segments of the society.

4. The Trust of Society

Between business and society the distrust index is very high. Society does not respect the corporate community and there is a general impression that the corporate community does not follow any ethics and their sole motive is to make money at any cost. This impression has to be changed. Capitalism with a human face means that social trust has to be established; human face cannot be established unless 'Money Nexus' which is basic in business relationships in capitalism is replaced by a 'socio-economic value nexus'. Trust should be considered an economic or business asset.

Even in Kautilya's *Arthashastra,* social trust has been considered as a guiding philosophy:

- Maximum production was not the supreme objective of the economic organisation.
- Commerce or wealth-making was not an end in itself. And merchants and manufacturers carried out their activities as a trust for the society they lived in.
- The healthiest state of affairs was one in which values higher than worldly possessions received honour and approval.

Capitalism / market economies can only flourish if socio-economic value creation is considered seriously, for only it can minimise social contradiction and reduce the distrust between society and business / corporate community. Social good does not come naturally to capitalism/market economies. Concerted efforts are required to be put so that society will accept the benefits and give credit to the corporate community for social good and hence start respecting it. Business has to move towards trust and transparency for its survival and growth. Without building social trust it will be difficult for the corporate community to have a meaningful existence.

Reports of corporate scandals, fraudulent activities, crime, greed, corruption, manipulation etc only increase social distrust. Corporate community should take necessary action collectively to control a handful of vulgar people or scoundrels who destroy the trust of society and increase social contradictions. A high-level government probe recently found Xerox Modicorp, a subsidiary of the US-headquartered copier major Xerox Inc., guilty of making "improper payments" for procuring sales both from government and private parties and ordered the formation of an inter-agency group, including the CBI, to determine the course of action against the firm. The investigation against the company was ordered in 2002 after Xerox Inc., admitted in a submission with the US Securities and Exchange Commission (SEC) that its Indian subsidiaries had made improper payments to get government orders worth Rs.3.5 crore. The company and its officials were charged with deliberate destruction of evidence under the provisions of the Indian Penal Code. Other violations included evasion of income tax, criminal conspiracy and aiding and abetting commission of offences.

According to a study, the poor traditionally trust corporations the least when it comes to environment, human rights and health. The media, the government and the NGOs follow in that order on their distrust index. This may be due to corruption, which increases income inequality, biased systems, poor targeting of social programmes, lobbying by rich for fabourable policies that perpetuate inequality in asset ownership, capture of public spending and unequal access to education. Social trust can be achieved by:

1. Taking concrete action to establish integrity, transparency in terms of social responsibility and social good which will be reflected in day-to-day activities of the corporate community.
2. Offering products or services free of superficiality in terms of:
   - Intrinsic value/utility
   - Quality
   - Price
   - Genuineness of product features which will make lives better and more comsfortable

In the ultimate analysis products / services should be offered with socio-economic insight and not on the basis of market share strategy, segmentation, branding, positioning theory, competition, ROI etc.

So many brands are failing because either customer or the society does not have trust. Trust has to be built, and without building trust the brand power cannot be utilised. As Peter Drucker mentioned recently, "Suppliers and especially manufacturers have information about a product or service that the customer does not have and cannot, and does not need if he can trust the brand. This explains the profitability of brands."

One recent example is when due to the pesticide controversy, the sale of Pepsi & Coke dropped substantially. As per some report, on an average, sales dropped 50-60% in several states, and still both the companies are still struggling to recover.

Zig Zigler identified five reasons why people do not buy: either because they didnot feel the need, or they were not in a hurry to buy, or had no desire,or money to buy the product. But the big reason why people did not consummate the deal was lack of trust.

5. Concern for environment

"Instead of clinging to a perspective focussed on regulatory compliance, companies need to ask such questions as -What are we wasting? And how could we enhance customer value?" Porter and Van der Linde.

Mahatma Gandhi said that economic development becomes relevant only when it is based on principles of enviromental conservation and harmony, and equity with justice. Genuine concern for environment is fundamental. Here compliance of the statutory laws / rules will not serve the real purpose.

Corporations and the corporate community should realise that addressing environmental issues is not only necessary but is a must to get the social trust in 21st century. If environmental issues are addressed creatively innovatively, this not only helps to achieve social trust but also increase effeciency, productivity and improves also the bottomline. Some of the companies have already introduced innovative procedures and have started getting the results.

Genuine commitment, effort, concrete planning and action are required. Environment management should not be considered as 'cost centre' it, but has to be in corporated in the socio-economic value creation proposition / model.

The mind-set has to be transformed from compliance to commitment. That's the key. We all know that the Bhopal tragedy has due to the calousness of the management and the negligence of the statutory authority. Several rules, regulations, laws and agreements / protocols have been introduced nationally and internationally.

In India main statutory laws/acts prevailing are:

- The Water(Prevention & Control of Pollution) Act, 1974.
- The Air(Prevention and Control of Pollution)Act, 1981.
- The Environment (Protection) Act, 1986.
- The Hazardous Wastes (Management & Handling) Rules, 1989.
- The Public Liability Insurance Act, 1991.
- The National Environment Tribunal Act, 1995.
- The Bio-Medical Wastes (Management & Handling) Act, 1998.
- Regulation of Recycling of Waste Oil and Non-ferrous Scrap, 1999.
- Ozone Depleting Substances (Regulation & Control) Rules, 2000. Commits countries to protecting the Ozone layer by controlling the release of CFCs and halons.
- Basel Convention: Governs generation, transportation and disposal of hazardous wastes across national boundaries.
- Kyoto Protocol: Offers a framework to address the causes of climate change; requires developed nations to reduce greenhouse gas emission.
- Convention on Biological Diversity: Seeks to ensure the conservation of biological diversity and the sustainable use of its components.
- Rotterdam Convention: Regulates the trade of 38 hazardous chemicals, requires exporting countries to get prior consent of the importing countries.

- POPs Convention: Also known as the Stockholm Convention, it bans the use of 12 "dirty chemicals"- like DDT.

In reality, rules / regulations have got a limited relevance. Ultimately, it boils down to the commitment and core values of the companies.

Despite the progress corporate sector has made over the last few years, a lot more remains to be done. Hazardous leakages or industrial accidents still occur with some frequency. In several companies the waste management system is outdated and in some cases even industrial effluents are being discharged in rivers without much control.

A large number of small and medium enterprises are not at all interested in efficient management of environment. Of course the corporate sector has started giving importance to environmental issues, compliance levels, benchmarking, and cetification like ISO14001 also have increased considerably but in reality commitment is lacking, it is still lip service or some how a way to satisfy the satutory authority.

Concern for environment has to be an integral part of the value system and the business model so that necessary investment and planning action can be taken innovatively. A reference guideline:

- Commitment beyond compliance
- Environment should be an integral part of socio-economic value creation proposition
- Integrity in compliance of regulations standards
- Genuine audit / certification / benchmarking
- Employee participation involvement
- Product design and facility design should be environment friendly by adopting best technology available in the market

- Best technology and procedure to be adopted in creatively managing waste, for by-product management and energy management.

The corporate sector also should try to educate , influence, motivate and guide the connected companies like suppliers of raw materials, providing other services and even member of industry as suggested by T. N. Khoshoo: "We need to usher in environmental education with regard to long-range ecological security. Natural, agro and industrial economic systems have to be both conserved and used in a sustainable manner. There has to be a healthy blend of environmental, social, developmental and economic imperatives. A sustainable society has faith in science and technology as an instrument of environment-friendly social and economic change-because economic growth should not be at the expense of ecological assets. We should work in partnership with nature and conserve non-renewable resources and energy and reduce wastage".

Strict accountability is a must. Health costs are hidden costs. They are never factored in when computing pollution costs. For implementation corporate sector has to take full responsibility.

Most Indian companies have not integrated environment management into their corporate strategy. Most of them look at ISO14001 certification as an end in itself, and the general mindset is to creatively manipulate the statutory authority. Most of the companies are focussing on compliance rather than creative or innovative strategies to create value.

There is no contradiction between a concern for environment and a sustainable business model. This is only a question of intention or core values.Environment issues should be considered as socio-economic value creation issues. This is also related to:

- Social trust
- Efficiency improvement
- Employees' morale

Environmental mishaps can seriously damage corporate reputations, impose heavy costs and, in extreme instances, even lead to bankruptcy. A good example is the Bhopal gas tragedy of 1984. Thousands of people lost their lives and many more were disabled and left homeless after methyl isocyanate gas leaked from the Union Carbide plant. Union Carbide 's reputation never recovered from this tragedy. Recently, Hindustan Lever Ltd has been involved in a mercury leakage incident at its Kodaikanal plant. Although the impact of the leakage on the environment seems to have been marginal, HLL has paid a heavy price in terms of both money and managerial resources after the incident was reported.

Environment concerns should become strategic concerns and should be integral parts of business models or strategy. Some people are suggesting, like the Energy Act of 2003, this should be made mandatory for companies to hire an environment officer or manager. Will it work? Unless corporate character is transformed; value creation model is changed and 'environment' is factored in the business model nothing substantial will be achieved. As M.C. Badarinarayana, advisor with SHE cell of the Bombay Chamber of Commerce & Industry observed: " Recycling an empty Pepsi can saves as much energy as used for three hours of TV-watching. Corporates must address environment questions from cradle to grave-from raw material procurement through production, distribution to dealer, retailer, and customers, and thereafter too. Still a far cry here."

To create socio-economic values, we have to convert company having limited liabilities into an "Institution" of socio-economic value creation responsibilities.

To bring ecological eqilibrium, an organisation should understand the relevance of the observations made by Satish Kumar in an recent interview: "Ecology is not against economy. The earth is a balanced system. The whole thing is like a dance-it has to go in steps. If something goes ahead, there is disruption. At the moment, there is no synchronisation. We need to realise that participation in the process of making is more important than consuming what is being made. In a quantitative society quality will be destroyed."

How many companies really respect the UN Charter for Nature : Life depends on the uninterrupted functioning of natural systems which ensure the supply of energy and nutrients. Civilisation is rooted in nature which has shaped human culture and influenced all artistic and scientific endeavour.

The four-year-long Millennium Ecosystem Assessment's Summary Report, the first comprehensive global bio-diversity evaluation programme and the biggest review of the planet's life support system recently published, says that humans have changed ecosystems more rapidly and extensively in the last 50 years than in any other period of their existence. Also that more land has been converted to agriculture since 1945 than in the 18th and 19th centuries put together, resulting in a substantial and largely irreversible loss in diversity of life on earth. Upto 30% of the mammalian, bird and amphibian species are currently threatened with total extinction. That's enough evidence for experts to warn of the likelihood of potentially abrupt changes which could seriously affect human well-being, including the emergence of new diseases, sudden changes in water quality, creation of "dead zones" along coastlines and shifts in regional climate. The assessment team warns that the ability of the earth's ecosystem to sustain future generations can no longer be taken for granted.

This is high time that we should wake up and introspect to take concrete actions to identify the changes in institutions and policies which are required to eliminate the main causes of environmental degradation.Kofi Annan,Secretary General of the UN rightly advised: "Only by understanding the environment and how it works, can we make the necessary decisions to protect it".

Tracing the idea of social good

The idea of socio-economic value creation is not new. Even in the ancient Indian value system the 'social good'was incorporated :

Satyam (truth) : which is the ethical component of business. Shivam (welfare) : which should be the economic objective of business. And Sundaram (Beauty) : which should be the aesthetical outlook like purity of ideas and morality in behaviour.

Kautilya's *Arthashastra* described the healthiest state of affairs was one in which values higher than worldly possessions received honour and approval, maximum production was not the supreme objective of the economic organisation, commerce or wealth making was not an end in itself; and merchants and manufacturers carried out their activities in a trust for the society they lived in.

Spiritualism or social philosophy as propagated by the Buddha, Sri Ramakrishna, Swami Vivekananda, Mahatma Gandhi and other great human beings also taught us the importance of social justice or socio-economic value creation. They taught us fundamental values of compassion, dignity of life, human and natural existence. Essence of their teachings is social good /transformation which can not be achieved without socio-economic value creation.

The idea of 'social good' had also been refected in the history of business development in America. Edward Filene represented a whole generation of progressive American businessmen who utilised their wealth and influence for a higher public purpose. In 1908 he set up the first Credit Unions in the United States. Today 76 million Americans belong to 11000 Credit Unions in the US. Another businessman, Andrew Carnegie, supported a whole range of philanthropies and foundations. One of his contributions, for example, was his endowment of $10 million in 1905, to create a pension for teaching in colleges and universities. He limited his pension to institutions that set a high academic bar, thus helping in raising the standards of higher education. His subsequent actions led to the creation of an annuity fund for teachers, which has now evolved into the TIAA-CREF, one of the largest insurance funds in the US.

Serious thinking in respect of 'social resposibility' or social good' as a part of business strategy started among a section of business community in US during 1980's. They started sincerely accepting that business should include other elements beyond making money effeciently. This concept got attention, when a host of companies started contributing for charity and started talking about social and ethical criteria in their business relationships. Others talked about the "double bottomline" i.e measuring not only profits but also the social and environmental impact of the business.

The ideas behind this thinking flowed into mainstream under the catchword "sustainability." John Browne, Chief Executive of BP Plc, talked about this in the world's second largest oil company's" 2003 Sustainability Report." To be sustainable," he wrote," a company cannot exist in isolation but must recognize and manage its wider impact and contribution to society. In otherwords, sustainability considers whether the business benefits the world in the long run,providing a product, service and shareholder return while also considering the impact on the environment, or society."

The crux of the matter is whether a company can pursue these goals of sustainability without sacrificing profits. Some companies, built with sustainability in mind at their inception, have found that the approach has been key to growth and profitability. An example is the La Farge, Wisconsin, a farming cooperative selling milk under the organic valley label, is the largest U.S enterprise of its kind. It was set up to provide a fair price to small farmers for their product, thereby providing economic sustainability in rural areas.

Value Generation Institution:

A value creating institution first and foremost has to internalize the invisible power of organizational mind and channelise this power for guiding all activities. They should believe value is created by people, around people and for the people. Organisation mind / Corporate character is the **context creating resource** which is to be liberated for proper utilisation.

Already realisation has started in corporate sector to accept that the shareholder is not first but the citizen or the country is. Commitment beyond stock market is essential for survival and growth. A recent advertisement by ITC limited- 'Citizen First' puts to focus on their commitment to society / country, and is a clear indication of the new realisation.

The same realisation is also reflected as Tarun Das, Director-General, CII, articulated in a recent article "...Industry has to change itself and its institutions from a mindset of being a trade union of employers to an organisation dedicated to development with a higher order of vision."

The concept of 'Citizen First' and the organisation should stretch for better future of the citizen- and this should be the central focus for socio-economic value creation.

Hiroyuki Yoshino, CEO, Honda Motors, rightly emphasized: "Through self–innovation, we should challenge ourselves to make our automobiles, motorcycles and power products cleaner and more efficient. In this way, we can provide our customers with the fun and excitement they have enjoyed in the past, while creating a better future for the environment and society." Socio-economic value creation should be the epicentre of all corporate activities and organisations should appreciate the **basics of value creation:**

- Citizen/society first
- Value created by people, around people and for the people

Today, all over the world, people are trying to address the critical issue of sustainability. The corporate sector has a special responsibility to contribute to this larger mission while achieving its business objectives. The corporate sector, while generating economic surplus, needs to sharpen its focus on replenishing natural capital and on eliminating poverty through the creation of sustainable employment opportunities. Jayant Sinha, partner with Mckinsey & Company observed in a recent article: "Great companies are vital for the growth of the Indian economy. First, they create hundreds of thousands of well-paying jobs. In turn, each of these jobs creates many other jobs—the driver, the ayah, the gardener, the vegetable supplier and so on-that provide services to the middle-class Indian family. Ten great companies can support five million families. Second, these companies force all their suppliers to improve their business practices raising productivity for the *keiretsu* or ecosystem and for the industry as a whole. Wal-Mart and Toyota have had exactly this impact on their suppliers."

Socio-economic value evaluation guide:

There cannot be any clear cut index or equation or guide to measure socio-economic value creation. However, the core group of the organisation should devise some guidelines to evaluate and monitor the value creation process. An example is mentioned here as a reference:

02 points scale has been considered where CF indicates completely fulfilled, PF indicates partially fulfilled and NF indicates not fulfilled. CF-2, PF-01 and NF-0.

Figure: 2 Value evaluation guide

Parameters	CF	PF	NF
Supply side	02		
Demand side		01	
Socio-cultural side			0
Social trust			
Environment concern			

The evaluation of the performance by the pre-determined guidelines should not be handed over to a 'third party' or auditor. Ownership of evaluation of performance has to be accepted by the core group and the core group should evaluate by themselves with a clear objective in mind.

3

Corporate Character

Minds are parachutes, they only function when open-

Thomas R. Dewar

The mind is an energy field; it allows you to go up and down. Knowledge gives you the insight to know the right direction to take but ultimately only wisdom helps you to choose.

Swami Sukhobodhananda

The empires of the future are the empires of the mind-

Winston Churchil

Character Matrix

Human Character is a very complex combination, interaction and synergy of various aspects / attributes such as:

- Values/beliefs
- Attitudes
- Honesty
- Commitment
- Conviction
- Courage
- Personality

Character impacts the effectiveness and contribution of a human being. In the ultimate analysis, like human being the 'Corporate character' also is the key driving force for all activities. Human systems depend on emotional capital and corporate character is a mechanism to create and sustain that capital. Corporate Character is shaped by the complex interaction and combination of the following:

1. Mind of the Organization

- Core values/purpose
- Context creating attributes/parameters

2. Corporate Personality

3. Core Group Alignment

An attempt has been made to analyse the essence and various attributes of 'Corporate Character' which can transform the balancesheet company into a socio-economic value creating institution.

1. Mind of the Organization

Mind is the mover and source of power

There is simply no limit to what man can achieve with the power of ideas or thoughts. An idea, a thought or a book can influence minds of others if it is powerful. More powerful the idea or thought more influence it wields among people and shapes their perceptions and consciousness or thinking process, notions and attitude, which in turn may shape the behaviour of individuals and the society in the direction desired by the thought or idea. All ideas or thoughts come from the mind only. Primary key of human efficiency, effectiveness and achievement is the MIND. Keynes, Karl Marx, Rabindranath Tagore, Swami Vivekananda, Einstein, Mahatma Gandhi, Nelson Mandela and several other great people made great contributions for mankind because of their mind, and not because of availability of material resources or otherwise. The history of human civilization shows that the, human mind is the prime mover for all achievement and creation. Mind is the epi-centre of all socio-economic value creation.

In the ultimate analysis the movement of the mind results in thoughts, words, actions, aspirations and achievements. Swami Vivekananda said: "All knowledge the world has ever received comes from the mind; the infinite library of the universe is in your own mind. The external world is simply the suggestion, the occasion, which sets you to study your own mind, but the object of your study is always your own mind. The falling of an apple gave the suggestion to Newton, and he studied his own mind; he re-arranged all the previous links of thought in his mind and discovered a new link among them which we call the law of gravitation. It was not in the apple nor in anything in the centre of the earth."

In history, we have seen how Emperor Asoka completely changed due to transformation of mind and contributed immensely for the emancipation of mankind by propagating peace and social harmony. Saint Valmiki wrote one of the most valuable books / epics due to transformation of his mind. Human mind which imagines, reasons and creates is dynamically active, and is playing a crtical role in the process of its own evolution and also in the survival of all living things. The future of our evolutionary course will be in the realm of psychic development, and new potentialities will make us surpass ourselves. Mind is the primary force in the world.

Mind plays a very important role from an economic activity -point of view also, as Keynes stated: "Apart from instability due to speculation, there is the instability (because) a large proportion of our activities depend on spontaneous optimism rather than mathematical expectations."

Animals are also living in this world but they are at the mercy of human beings because they do not have mind power. Hence, they are not able to create,change and control their 'Living Condition'.

The so-called 'Human Resource Management' is a misnomer. Resource by definition is dead, it has to be exploited, utilized and transformed for value addition. Human resource is not dead, it is a living thing and properties of human resource are not constant because a human being is guided by the mind. Potential of this resource is unlimited unlike other resources. Other resources are being utilized by human beings only. Even the robot and super computer are created by human beings through use of mind power.

Hence human resource cannot be defined by the same yardstick or treated like an other resource, and should not be considered as input of production. No other inputs are living and dynamic in nature. No other resource is having a mind.

Like cricket, business also in the ultimate analysis is a mind game. You may have the best batting line, bowlers, fielders but during the actual game players are failing to perform due to problems in mind as Mark H. McCormack said: "The champion's true edge exists solely in the mind." A top-ranking tennis star would mentally switch off all other factors—previous losses against the opponent, track record on that surface, and so on and focus only on the game, putting the pressure of winning /losing out of his mind, thereby naturally executing those breathtaking shots even in extremely tight situations which most of us can replicate in practice sessions. Read reports of matches involving the world's best players and you find repeated references to the fact that they play the 'big points' better than the rest. The simple reason for this is that they just don't see those situations as 'big points' while their 'under-pressure' opponents are wary of committing an unforced error at a crucial stage, they just play their natural game and move in for the kill.

Inspite of availability of huge medical facilities, doctors and medicines, people are having diseases and are suffering. Human ability depends on the mind. Only the mind can regulate individual lifestyle, exercise, food habit, accept of pressure, sexual stability etc. no amount of psychologist / health guru's advice can help Dr. V. K. Nigam, a renowned Surgeon in an interview explained the importance of mind:" I have faith in allopathy, we now know everything about the body. But the treatment must be about the mind as well. This is where I feel prayer comes in...........I pray for healt, happiness, wisdom, peace and contentment .... prevention is very important. But let's face it, people do fall ill. We need to manage illness not through surgical intervention as the first option, but through lifestyle changes and meditation."

Human potential is unlimited. You see the great singers, composers, sportpersons, writers, architects and business leaders-—all have achieved because of their mind and not because of resources being available or not available.

'The world is not understood by contemplation but by action' and for action, mind is the mover and source of power. Even if all factors of resources are given one cannot be a world class sportsperson or great writer unless the mind is accepting the challenges and becomes determined to achieve.

A Harvard University study indicates that information accounted for only 15%. Attitude contributed the rest. Modern education, however, is almost entirely focussed on facts and figures. We should focus on attitude and inner working of the mind. It helps to improve skills and also re-engineer our inner personality. The higher we go the greater is the role played by our mind. It's mind alone that separates a great hopeful from a great achiever. "Your attitude, not your aptitude, will determine your altitude" says Zig Zigler.

Relevance of organisation mind

An organization is a going concern and it is like a living entity. It has to work in a dynamic complex world like human existence. Business economic entity are facing tremendous complex and dynamic environments in terms of politics, economics, trade, technology, market, customers, competition, international and global economy etc.

No computer model can give the dynamism, no CEO can ensure the full utilization of an organisation's potential, no management guru, management schoool and school of economics can help. Dynamic situation is so complex that no theory and model can help you to take decisions or make strategies.

We have seen the death of the so-called "excellent companies" inspite of the fact that several management gurus, consulting firms and management schools are working. This is a paradox. Even some of the consulting firms are struggling to survive and some of the management schools are also performing very badly.

Several countries in the world are also struggling to survive. Some are living virtually at the mercy of the big countries. So many economic pundits are available. So many nobel laureates are available even then the situation is extremely bad. Several hundred crores people are just living without any dignity and are waiting for the charity of the socalled NGOs and for running these NGOs there are consultants. There are several top schools of economics—who are producing so-called economists and hundreds of theories, models principles are being introduced but the ground reality remains that 60 % of humanity is in absolutely miserable situation.

Like in a human being transformation of the country depends on the country's mind or on the Average Social Consciousness. Swami Vivekananda rightly said:" The rise of nations comes with an increase of men of character and of strong ethical and moral fibre." So called economists/ management gurus or NGOs will be of no use unless the character is transformed.

As per a World Bank report, massive growth of local NGOs in developing countries has not been effective in reducing proverty. During the nineties,the number of local NGOs in India increased to one million—there is one local NGO for every thousand people. However, the proverty situation has not changed much. Around 1980 when various techno-managerial NGOs emerged on Indian scene, it looked as if the NGOs would replace the government bureaucracy in so far as development administration is concerned. But this myth was broken within a decade. Lack of rule of law, lack of sound project management and aspiration to become an alternative bureaucracy with a five-star culture shattered the myth. Several NGOs had to be black listed. The development NGOs developed but the people for whom they were working did not develop as desired.

For a unit either individual, family, club, social or religious group, team, company or corporation - the mind is required to be transformed, changed and utilized. In that sense this is universally applicable. However, in this book focus will be on 'Organisation Mind dynamics / transformation'- parameters and implications.

Nothing is perfect in this world. No organization will ever be perfect. However, no organisation will be able to withstand the shock of the reality unless they transform their balancesheet mindset to a value generation mindset. This is a must irrespective of 'size' of the company for survival in the twenty-first century. The company's vision, mission, objectives and goals etc will remain as politically correct a statement, and on paper or display board only. This will be too abstract and irrelevant for the employees or public at large.

Like the mind controls the human performance,similarly organization mind controls and contributes for the well being of the company. Computer hardware is meaningless without appropriate software. Similarly any country's development depends on the mind of the country i.e average consciousness of the citizen and the society. Within the past several years, we have seen some organizations flourish, others subsist and yet others on the brink of collapse. Although, to some extent the fortunes of organizations are determined by outside environmental forces, in a good part, an organisation's success is a product of its internal functioning which in the ultimate analysis depends on 'organisation mind' dynamics.

Why a dead body is of no use? Because it has lost the spirit energy or the mind though it has all the physical parts available. Similarly without the proper mind an organization is like a dead body. All physical assets will not be of any use. No technology, plant, process, strategy, policy, advertisement, brand management and PR will help. Sri Ramakrishna rightly taught us: "Bondage is of mind and freedom is also of the mind."

There is no intention to write any new concept or theory. These are already existing in one form or the other. Only it is tried to impress upon that we can't build great institutions without having great minds like the human being. Without soci-economic value creation, organisations will face tremendous difficulty in surviving in the 21st century. As rightly observed by Ray Irani, CEO, Occidental petroleum : "Success for a oil and gas company in the 21st century means working in harmony within diverse political, cultural and geographic environments. It means providing a safe and healthy workplace for employees, serving as responsible stewards of the environment, being a good neighbour to communities near your operations, and maintaining the highest standards of ethical behaviour."

Some basic observations from personal experience of various companies including some Fortune 500 companies:

- Irrespective of the size those companies are following 'balancesheet approach'.
- Huge wastage of resources—opportunity cost.
- Huge disguised under-utilization of human capability.
- No genuine respect for human beings or customers- 'People' is missing in the whole scheme of things.
- CEO / promoters believe company is progressing or performing due to ' 70% vision of the CEO / Promoters, 20 %Technology and 10% inspite of people.'
- Manipulative, bureaucratic, feudal atmosphere-"cat is black or white does not matter" kind of mindset.
- No concern for ethics / integrity.
- Profit is central to all activities.
- Greed has become the invisible creed or core value.
- Top management is always busy in maximising their personal agenda.

Balancesheet discloses/displays what managements want it to. It hides more than it discloses. If you go by the balancesheet these are supposed to be big companies and doing well but they have failed to become great instituitions which inspire not only their employees but the public at large. We have to differentiate between a balancesheet company and a great institution which inspires and contributes. We have the recent example of Enron, World Com, Tyco, AOL- big balancesheet companies collapsed within no time. We have read the recent story of GTB also.

The main difference between a balancesheet company and the institution is that the former is concerned about the number in the balancesheet, while the institution genuinely believes that value is created by the people, around people and for the people. To achieve this, the transformation of the organization mind is a must.

Several companies and B-schools have started realising the importance of 'mind / character'. Some companies are organising spirituality and yoga classes for the employees. Some of the B-schools introduced spirituality as a subject. Though there are differences in opinion regarding the importance of spirituality in business but the whole objective is to transform the mind and character. Mainly these reasons are cited:

1. In 21st century an organisation needs to innovate continuously to survive and grow for which every employee including the top management in the organisation needs to leverage his creative energy by connecting to God's Own creative energy.
2. So many scandals,corporate mis-conduct, fraudulent activities are happening because of inappropriate value system.
3. Corporate governance can not be ensured without following proper value system.
4. To achieve the individual's mental stability which is required to concentrate in today's complex,competitive and stressful environment.

Organisation mind: the invisible power

Organisation mind cannot be defined in a very precise and structured manner. Like human mind organisation mind is also quite complex and which is a combination of so many factors /parameters/attributes and interactions, interrelationship and the ultimate outcome of all these factors determines the organisation /corporate mind dynamics. Like the human mind the corporate mind is also some kind of Black Box which cannot be analysed / comprehended in a precise manner like mathematics. However, every organization should try to understand the basics of the organization mind in order to utilize the effectiveness of the company for value creation.

As we know a toxic mind can only destroy the human intelligence. Similarly toxic mind of the organization destroys the capability of the organization and cannot become an institution which can continuously generate value and withstand the market dynamics.

Like the human mind the organization mind is invisible yet is the most powerful. This power can be channelised in a negative or postive manner. Any company / organisation which wants to be an institution this mind power is to be internalized, explored and practised and utilized in a real sense not in a superficial way. Organisations should realise : 'Dreams get done when you are transparent in your intentions.'

By a proper study of the corporate mind we can understand the internal dynamics and its relation to external forces and thereby we can avoid misplaced optimism on few individuals based on corporate / organizational power structure /equations. Invisible power is the driving force of all achievement and activity.

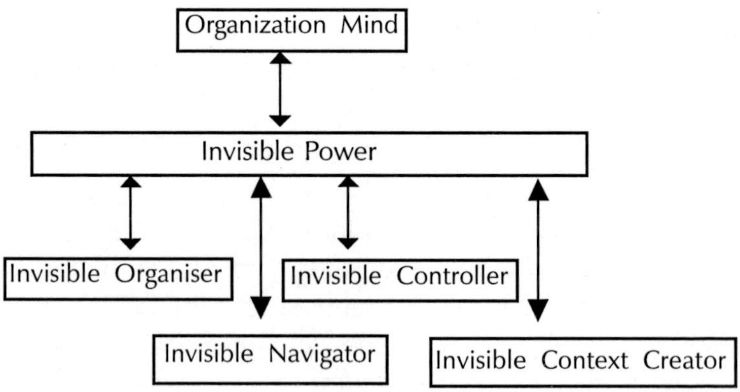

Fig 3.1: An architectural view of organisation mind

Invisible organiser	:	Organise all activities/ plans & programmes
Invisible navigator	:	Direct and navigate through different processes/paths
Invisible controller	:	Review, monitor and control as per core values/purpose. Act as inner eye.

Invisible context

Context cannot be defined in exact terms since this is invisible and unwritten. This is the average collective perception and feeling of the working situation. Context cannot be measured

or quantified since this is a process , perception / and feeling not a thing. Context is not static. It is dynamic and is always in an evolutionary stage. It's direction and conduciveness and quality are to be maintained by constant effort. Context always depend on time,space and people. This is the result of complex combination and interaction of of the following main aspects:

- Average collective consciousness.
- Average collective commitment to values /ethics / fair practices.
- Average collective behaviour which creates situation and facilitates for creative contribution by the team as well as the individual.
- Situation which unshackles people's innate and spontaneous intelligence, creates the context for creation of value and contribution by individual as well as utilization of organizational resources.

Human being is context specific:

Except human beings all other resources are context neutral. Other resources do not have mind and are not affected by the context. Context is to be created to utilize the potential of the human resource to utilize other resources, and motivate and engage the people to create new value out of socio-economic resources /opportunities continuously, and to achieve a higher level of value creation.

Overall experience of values, transperancy, creativity and fostering ignites the genius of the employees. People cannot just go off and design the experience they inherit it. It's conversations, oral tradition and leading by example. The source of people's action in the work place isn't what they know but how they perceive the organisation. Creating context is a completely different thing to work on than knowledge, information and other resources.

In human life, no book, text, theory or concept is permanent. All aspects of human life are context specific or depend on context.Context is supreme. Vidyut Joshi observed in an article *'Learning to Live Together'*:".....As such life does not have a meaning but you can give it a meaning. So the meaning of life could vary according to the context. People live in different time and space contexts. They have different experiences; so they give different meanings to their lives and try to realise those meanings. Whether that is true or false is a different matter."

Core values :Core of the organisation mind

Institutions are those that possess core values and a core purpose which remain unaltered while their business strategy and practices endlessly adapt to a changing world.

Core values/purpose of a socio-economic value generation institution:

- Sincerely believe that value is created by the people, around the people and for the people
- Sincerely believe: 'organisation is the partner of the society.' As a human being cannot survive without society, similarly no organisation can survive and grow and become an institution without becoming the partner of the society.
- Are Inspired by the larger picture of reputation and recognition-and respected / accepted as a socio-economic value creator who contributes to improve quality of life in a continuous way.
- Constant search for innovation / creativeness and equipping the organization with better resources for improving the capacity to create socio-economic value.
- Demonstrate discipline in its activities and be inherently accountable for its actions and influence the external environment by its positive and proactive acts and becoming inspiration for others.
- Genuinely believe in trust,transparency and integrity.

Core value / guiding principle should be considered as ATMA. Core values are like divine light. Any company wanting to become an institution, has to move and flow with the divine light i.e core values.

Core values work as a 'stabilising force' in midst of so much complexity, confusion, and uncertainties in both internal and external environment of the company. Core values are enduring of time and space. Values provide a clear framework within which corporate decisions and activities are carried out. Core values are the basis to create a context for an outstanding innovation / creativity and execution, for socio-economic value creation or to provide product or services with socio-economic solutions or insights.

Xray of corporate mind : Context creating attributes

Like the human mind, the organisation mind is also a black box, too complex and abstract. However, an attempt has been made to understand the basics of the oranisation mind which can transform the organisation's character to create value for the organisation and the society.

Figure: 3.2 Context creating parameters

No.	Parameter		No.	Parameter
1.	Concern for ethics/ integrity		17.	Concern for valu creation
2.	Cultivate excellence		18.	Constant & Open Communication
3.	Cultivate continuous learning		19.	Creating caring context
4.	Creativity & Innovation		20.	Concern for details
5.	Channeling intellectual diversity		21.	Cultivate inspiration capital
6.	Commitment		22.	Competence
7.	Concern for society/country		23.	Concern for people
8.	Connectivity to market/ society	CORE VALUES	24.	Consider human talent as capital
9.	Concentration		25.	Concept of feudalism
10.	Create dreams		26.	Concern for quality
11.	Convert dreams into reality		27.	Cultivateaction orientation
12.	Change orientation		28.	Concern for equilibrium/ unity
13.	Collective & Collaborative wisdom		29.	Consistency
14.	Complacence		30.	Comfort for failure
15.	Clear sense of direction		31.	Constructive dissent
16.	Consultation		32.	Consider time as input

1. Concern for ethics/integrity

No great institution can be built without the concept of ethics or value system. You will not find a single great human being whose activities where not based on a concept of ethics. Swami Vivekananda once said "No great things can be achieved with cleverness." Imperialism / fascism have collapsed, most powerfull dictator have been thrown out. Concept of ethics / integrity is universal, applicable for individual, organization and the country. So many big companies collapsed like a pack of cards was not due to lack of resources but lack of concern for ethics. In the long run 'cleverness' does not pay. Cleverness is accompanied by deceit and often, blatant lies. People see through this. The company, therefore should operate sincerely and smartly, not cleverly.

To make a great instituition, management should no longer accept the premise that the only objective of the business / company is to make profit by any means. Though without profit the firm will not exist and will eventually have to shut shop, it is now also accepted that the primary purpose of a business is to create and retain customers and build a relationship which matures with each passing day and by which trust and confidence are forged between an organization and the customers. True, profit is as necessary to a business enterprise as food is necessary to sustain human or animal life. But by the same criterion, he would be foolish who says that he lives only to eat. What is true for individuals is also true for a business entity.

Corporate landscape is full of scandals, unethical behaviour, corporate misconduct, fradulent activities and transaction. Recent classic examples are –Enron / World Com, AOL, Tyco, GTB and in all cases CEOs, CFOs and other top management people have been involved who are supposed to be highly educated and so, intelligent. There should be a commitment from the top people towards ethics / integrity and for not allowing greed to become the organisational creed or core value. 'Fish rotten from the head'-is as true an adage for the organisations also.

There are some people who suggest that, given the socio-economic environment it is not possible to ensure integrity but they are advised to remember the observation made by Jeffrey

Egarten, Dean of the Yale School of Management, in his book, *The Politics of Fortune: A New Agenda for Business Leaders*: "The essential point should not be lost: The more complex the markets become, the more the integrity of its leaders matters, and the less likely that higher prescriptive laws and regulations will really matter."

No self-respecting individual likes to work for an unethical organisation. Organisations can not be run by a command and control system. Excellence can be created and sustained by the employees who are inspired and motivated by values.

Integrity has to be appreciated, practised and nurtured by the core team of the organisation. Integrity should be the guiding parameter for the core team-then only this can become the integral part of organisational process and will be practised throughout the whole organisation. Subroto Bagchi rightly observed in an article: "This creates significant challenges for organisations that value integrity and expect their people to be principled-personally and professionally. The challenge becomes: how do you communicate a code of conduct to a fellow worker who is seeing the positional fall of government, big business and organised religion? Posters and first-day assimilation do not work any more. The only option, and a difficult one, becomes : walk the talk and talk the walk. First, people in position of influence have to demonstrate integrity, and then personally communicate the message to their organisation."

2. Cultivate excellence

'Cultivate excellence' is a guiding force and a unifying chord. Concern for excellence should be inherent in the organisation's context-from core people to the lowest employees should genuinely believe in excellence and consider that there is no 'finish line' in the pursuit of excellence.

Excellence should be considered as a process which has to be continuously improved and redefined. The whole organisation collectively should be committed to excellence and excellence is to be considered as a guiding philosophy. Imprints of excellence should be in every activity of the organisation if it wants to become an institution:

- Socio-economic value creation
- Application of technology
- Quality
- Integrity
- Trust
- Employee development

Excellence is not only comparing with the competitors or following global standards, also the organisation has to create new standards which others will follow—this should be the spirit.

'Cultivate excellence' means elimination of arrogance and complacence in a real sense and is always believing that things can be done in a better or a more creative way. Excellence ultimately depends on attitude as mentioned by Lou Holtz: "Ability is what you're capable of doing. Motivation determines what you do. Attitude determines how well you do it."

3. Cultivate continuous learning

Data, information, knowledge per se is dead. These become inputs when they are used for value creation, increasing efficiency and effectiveness of the organisation. For continuous creative or purposeful use of information, data, knowledge-organisation has to create context for utilisation of information,data and knowledge for value creation and also learn 'how to use knowledge' continuously. This is only possible when the whole organisational context facilitates this learning approach.

In a complex uncertain dynamic situation-'continuous learning' is the cutting edge. Existing data,information and knowledge only help in developing the ability to comprehend or understand the trend in technology, socio-economic variables, customer preferences, competitors' activities, financial market dynamics, political changes and international market dynamics etc.in order to decide business strategy and tactics.

Knowledge cannot be managed. It is too dynamic. The important issue is to learn how to use knowledge. Knowledge about application of knowledge / information / data will be a critical input to create socio-economic value in a sustained manner and get a competitive advantage in the 21st century.

4. Creativity/innovation

"Creativity involves breaking out of established patterns to look at things in a different way."- says Edward De Bone.

If an organization really wants to have a cutting edge, it has to respect innovators / risk takers and the creativeness of people so that they can flourish and contribute. Human existence and progress from time immemorial is nothing but the result of human creative mind. If you take the world as one unit, crores of people have contributed through their creative mind to the progress of human civilization. The countries which could successfully integrate and channelise human creativity and create the cultural context have developed tremendously, irrespective of the size and availability of resources.

Computer, telephone, mobile, TV, robot, language and all types of organizations are created by human beings. One CEO/MD (who may be too brilliant) becomes absolutely irrelevant for creative organization. They should play the role of integrators and create contexts to facilitate contribution by the individual. Is their any econometric model / computer model or software which can give strategy, create new ideas or give decision or commitment?

Creativity can be negative in nature also. Creativity should be directed towards a positive path for the benefit of customers and the society at large.

Managerial response to change must be through innovations/creativeness. Creativeness requires knowledge and understanding of the environment. Matched against this knowledge and understanding is the need for the evolution of the organizational core values and criteria that must be examined with respect to a never-ending time dimension.

Management should innovate to solve problems—problems in the sense of untapped opportunities-and not just to tide over immediate difficulties. True innovative or creative responses will have to stem from the desire and willingness to satisfy the needs of the teams or various diverse groups. Creative response does not mean merely introducing new systems, machines, technology or hiring consultants or recruiting some experts. Much more is involved. We need innovations / creativity to change and changes to create / innovate. The circularity of internal dynamics and external forces and circularity of change and creativity are to be understood properly.

As competition in the integrated global economy becomes sharper, problems become more complex, and as knowledge expands, one would expect that organizations would have to place more emphasis on planning for creativity / innovation. This implies planning goals which call for a stretch, creating flexible policy guidelines to channelise thinking without stifling imagination, designing roles where trans-disciplinary organizational team members can be creative, keeping updated about the trends in the external environment, and recognizing the urgency and expediency of channeling organizational policy and action towards desired outcomes. Innovation is the key driving force as Kiron Karnik wrote in an article *'Igniting Innovation For Growth'* :"....In tomorrow's world it is innovation that will drive corporate profits as well as national economies. Economic stardom will go to innovators."

Ideas make nations / corporations powerful. This can change the organisation and the country. No organisation can grow and create value without creativity / innovation / ideas. There should be a cultural propensity to lead than to follow. If we analyse the patent score card or innovation, India's performance is pathetic. Very few of India's big corporations have invested in projects outside their current service lines. There is no gameplan for creativity / innovation. Effort is to be made to facilitate an innovation-driven context propensity to value creation by creating a platform of competence or innovative capacity. This is possible through internal co-operation of various aspects of organisation's mind-human talent and context.

Innovative responsiveness will be the primary requirement in the 21st century. Contribution towards society must be through new ideas, and creative / innovative solutions. Creativity and innovativeness require deep knowledge and understanding of the complexity of the environment. As George Kneller said: "Creativity, as has been said,consists largely of rearranging what we know in order to find out what we do not know. Hence, to think creatively, we must be able to look afresh at what we normally take for granted."

This knowledge and understanding should be aligned with the core values / purpose /priorities of the company and the process is required to be reviewed continuously for proper implementation. Context is to be created to encourage and motivate all employees to innovate to solve problems-not only immediate difficulties but also to find out new opportunities for value creation.

Innovative or creative responses should become the part and parcel of the corporate character. It should not become just lip service by introducing some new procedure, new jargon or hiring consultants. It should become the mantra for addressing the problem, the whole organisation has to align and sincerely believe in innovation and creativity. It should become integral part of the planning process and every body should be involved and collaborate across the departments.

A context is to be created where innovation-both creation and diffusion- will be facilitated, and also encouragement/ appreciation of innovation as most vital to socio-economic value creation, for creating innovative, commercially viable and socially beneficial businesses and not to do current jobs more cheaply but to generate new products and services which will benefit the civic community the country. Innovation and creativity are about thinking of future opportunities rather than solving yesterday's consumer needs or problems.

Creativity is the ability to create ideas and innovation is a process to internalize the idea and create value for the customer / organization through viable business models. In the 21st century organization, product or services cannot survive meaningfully without creative / innovative character of the organization. The whole organization should be engaged in this sphere i.e all aspects of the organizational activities sales, production, R&D, customer service, marketing, planning, quality, product design, logistics, distribution etc.

Smart pricing strategy, brand or positioning strategy cannot ensure the bottomline any longer. Recent examples are HLL,

P&G, Pepsi / Coke : their pricing strategy, brand strategy did not really worked. Creativity / innovation is the key differentiator for value creation. Value can be created if creativity / innovation is focused on:

- Understand the socio-economic realities
- Understanding how knowledge/information can be channelised for value creation
- How best the technology can be used.
- How technology can be used to provide genuine utility/ convenience to a large number of people.

Purposeful creativity / innovation is socio-economic value-centric- and not for creating junk advertisement, manipulative strategy to make cosmetic changes in packaging, brand name-management for they are nothing but superficial creativity. Innovation / creativity should always be directed towards socio-economic value creation not to manipulate the market or innocent customers. All creative product / service solutions should be based on or rooted in the socio-economic reality. Innovation should not only touch a large number of lives but also bring about tremendous value. Innovation is not a one-time affair. It should been on-going-process. Innovation should offer a viable business solution also.

Innovation-incremental discontinuous should not be leader— centric-it should be socio-economic value-centric. It should not be organizational structure centric also. No organization sructure/system can ensure innovation for the society. Creativity is not the monopoly of any individual or group. It depends on the mind which is open and liberated from the thinking within the familiar 'box'. The mind should not be restricted by any particular subject / parameter, it has to move beyond the obvious and see the other areas to really understand the problems and find out solutions, for as Enrich

Fromn said : "Creativity requires the courage to let go of certainties."

Innovation does not necessarily always have to bea big bang. Many a times it may be choosing simple things and doing them well so that the organisation can become more effective and efficient.

The key driving force is the character of the corporation which creates the context.

5. Channeling intellectual diversity

In any organisation the biggest challenge is using the intellectual diversity. Diversity is about having different people looking at a problem differently or having different points of view for a particular solution to a problem. Diversity does not come automatically. It has to be appreciated and channelised for the benefit of the organisation. True spirit is to be cultivated as Mao Zedong once said: "Let a hundred flowers bloom,let one hundred schools of thought contend."

As per some study, a highly diverse group usually struggles more than a moderate group to arrive at regular results. The moderate groups get the regular results with a far higher consistency. But they do not get the breakthroughs. It is the diverse group that consistently generates significant breakthrough in ideas. As per the study there are three forms of diversity in managing complex work situations:

- Social identity diversity
- Informational diversity
- Values diversity

As per the study,social diversity on the basis of the obvious differentiators like race, gender, language, habits etc, is the least important,while the other two—informational diversity and values diversity—are more relevant for superior performance in group decision making. Informational diversity refers to differentiators like knowledge, skills, experience and background.

The same set of information is delivered differently and even acted upon differenly because its respective values offer different perspectives.

India as a country, is highly diverse with people from different places, with different habits, languages and cultures. Having natural diversity, and organisation has to encourage and utilise this diversity. This is critical as we begin to work in a globalised world. Every Indian company is becoming global in a big way. Their employees will have to deal with multi-national work groups more and more. And this is a strength we should capitalise. We have to sincerely encourage diverse thinking. Some of our educational & professional institutions have already proved the advantage accrued from natural diversity of India. They have become very successful since they bring together students and teachers who have grown up and studied in different parts of the country. That diversity then brings out quality in different ways in terms of competing with each other.

Organisation should celebrate and encourage intellectual diversity and not try to get everyone to think and work in the same way. Steven R Covey says:"...The key is to stop cloning others and start valuing differences....you may get some artificial harmony, comformity or uniformity (from cloning), but you won't have much creativity, synergy, unity or security."

Diversity is the key for innovation. We have to create a context that keeps the organisation innovative which will give that differentiating edge. We have to make people innovative and competitive through diversity.

"Our experience has been that a heterogeneous mix of people, though very difficult to lead, helps in the process of change.......Bringing in people from organisations with different cultures can be useful, so long as they all bond with the basic values of the organisation. So, moving away from homogeneity or creating an organisational climate that embraces different cultures and gives them wings whilst keeping the organisation rooted in its core values can be productive exercise and a useful catalyst in the change process." Says Kumarmangalam Birla, in an article 'How the Birla Group Transformed Itself.'

6. Commitment/passion

No individual can achieve anything without sincere commitment. No country can progress without the commitment of the leadership. Similarly, an organization can not progress or perform without the commitment of top management and employees and in terms of:

- Creating context.
- Ethics.
- Respecting creativity
- Respect for customer sensitivity
- Social good
- Core values

Continuous socio-economic value creation can be achieved only when organisations' employees and leadership acquire a higher value of delivery commitment. The context is to be created so that the whole organisation is engaged in acquiring higher value of delivery commitment through continuous improvement of socio-economic value creation capability.

Research on the psychology of groups has found 'task commitment' to be the common denominator for high performing groups—whether in the business world, military, sports or in voluntary organisations. Task commiment simply put is the commitment to do one's best and attempt the extraordinary. The distribution of task commitment in a group affects the performance of the group because it does not help if there is only one member of the group who is committed with the others being mere passengers or passive followers. The distribution of task commitment also influences social and informational forms of diversity.

"Men can practice skills for eight hours a day and that allows them to make a living. If they practice will for the remaining 16 hours that allows them to shape life. When skill and will come together in a cataclysmic moment, you unleash on to the world a 24-hour champion." Says Zig Ziglar and his advice is quite relevant.

Organisation must have the collective commitment or passion for socio-economic value creation. Passion is a gift of the spirit. It endows each of us with the power to live and communicate with unbridled enthusiasm. It is true for an individual as well as an organisation. Passion is most evident when the mind, body and spirit work together to create, develop and articulate or manifest our feelings, ideas and most sacred values for individual as well as organisation.

Passion enables us to overcome obstacles and to see the world as a place of infinite potential. The passionate spirit looks at every occurrence and every problem as an opportunity.Passion also has its own energy - an energy that's observable and transferable.

Passion cannot be created superficially. It has to come from heart and mind. Almost anyone, with only a bit of intuitiveness, can understand the hypocrisy or superficiality. That is why passion is such a powerful litmus in determining the authenticity of an individual, an organisation, a product or service. It supersedes the allure of expensive packaging. It makes transparent the hype of marketing mavericks and branding gimmicks. It strips away the thin veneer that separates what is said and what really is.

7. Concern for society and country

There is a general belief among the corporate community that they are in business only to make money and not for social service. No organization can flourish in the long run without the trust and goodwill from the society / country. Market means human beings society. Products or services ultimately will be sold in the market. If the country progresses and the society is developed automatically business will flourish. Hence the organization should try to paticipate in the activities for social /economical good of the people. Organisations should relate economic functions / activities with the socio-economic issues of the nation as a whole. Such responsiveness is required to build a great institution.

Nowadays lot of debate is going on regarding the concept of social responsibility. Three main prevalent approaches are :

- **Legal approach**: As per contract the company is having limited liability only towards shareholders.Business of business is business.
- **Hypocritical approach** : Pseudo- concern for society by donation or opening a charitable trust or during natural calamities do something for publicity purpose only.
- **Audit approach** : CSR concept –Trying to introduce some kind of index as an audit tool for public relation exercise.

Because of these approaches we are confused and miss the real issues. What is a company or organisation? Let us understand this first. From Keynes to Karl Marx to Peter Drucker to Kotler—companies exist because of value creation by the people and for the people. Organisation has to operate in the context of society and country.

Demand does not come from the sky; it has to be generated by the customer i.e people. No company can survive without the survival of people, society & country. This is the fundamental basis of any organization. Like individuals organization also cannot survive without society. This is a question of survival not responsiblity. An Institution has to be genuinely concerned for the society. It is not giving donation, opening schools, temples hospitals. Social responsibility should not be confused with charity. It should be based on compassion not pity. As Osho Rajneesh wrote in his book *'Osho's War and Peace : Insight from the Bhagavad Gita'* : "A compassionate person does not want there to be a single beggar on the face of this earth, but a man of pity wants beggars to exist, otherwise he will be in difficulty. Societies based on the concept of pity don't eradicate begging, they flourish it. If a compassionate society can be created, it won't be able to tolerate begging—it should not exist!"

From Keynes to Karl Marx, value has to be created and distributed. If there is no demand how will the value be created. For demand there has to be a disposable income with the people. Credit cards cannot ensure sustained demand in the market place. This is fundamental. We have seen several companies are struggling because the rate of growth of new people coming in the marketplace is much less than the so called expectation models of the companies. Companies are having marketing warfare among themselves to retain customers and improve the market share.

From experience we have seen that there is a huge wastage of resources in most of the companies. CEOs / top managements / promoters are simply siphoning funds or getting compensation which is totally disproportionate to their contribution and there is a huge difference between a lower level employee and the promoters / CEOs. The extravagant lifestyle, wastage, ineffciency and corruption are the silent killers of organisational capability. Even if the 500 major companies reduce their wastage by 10% several crore new customers can come in the market place. It is high time to establish some kind of rationality in terms of contribution and compensation. Several promoters /CEOs / top management always give mouthful of lecture to employees to think 'out of the box'. But when it comes to their facility /compensation and privileges they are only comfortable to think 'within the box'. This is a great hypocrisy.

Some economists / theoriticians are trying to sell the 'wealth /value creation concept': shareholder value maximization through market capitalisation. But what about loan / debt? Several promoters have taken loans from various banks and due to their callousness, corruption, cheating / siphoning of funds all have become bad debts. We want to take all sort of advantages from the society / country but when it comes to contribution to society we are trying to confuse by saying limited liabilities towards shareholders. Enron is a classic case of how a balancesheet company can cheat the people. The recent GTB case was another classic example of this kind.

8. Connectivity to market society

Sincere connectivity to the dynamics of reality is very important to understand the real feedback. Capability is to be developed to connect and respond to domestic and global environment. There are people who generally either justify the present situation due to their ignorance or are too complacent. They do not have the attitude / gut feeling to face the reality. To understand the reality an organisation must appreciate :

- Clear mind
- Critical observation

- Criticism
- Control ego of the core group

"Last mile connectivity"-this is the term used in telecom /infocom sector nowadays. No bandwidth, technology and investment will help unless you have last mile connectivity with the final customers. No organization can become institution unless having last mile connectivity with employees, customers and society at large.

Business model / strategy should be based on socio-economic value creation parameters. For socio-economic value creation deep insights are required:

- Cutomers 'lives or standard of living
- Social-cultural perspective
- Macro-economic variables
- Understanding of technology
- Environmental variables/issues

Deep insights come from keen observations of life and a search for deeper consumer truths with wider interpretation and relevance to life is needed. Superficial observations will not serve the purpose at all. Current mindsets or Market Research or other research methodologies are required to be re-visited and reinvented. It is best done by establishing a multifunctional team comprising of diverse background people to undertake this role in a continuous manner. This team has to interact and scan the environement to understand the socio-economic issues and advise the relevant product or services or ideas or changes to be made in offering.

Understanding socio-economic value creation should not be the prerogative of marketing department or product or brand managers or CEOs. The whole organisation should be committed in understanding the socio-economic issues and fulfilling the expectation of the society.

Several companies are facing difficulty in the market place due to lack of last mile connectivity. A large population is still outside the market system. How will the companies continuously achieve the "critical mass"? This is an illusion. You have to bring the majority of population in the market system by removing distortion and making the market transparent. 'India Shining'–a beautiful catchy slogan-but only for debating. India is shining only in the drawing room of the so-called intellectual having no connectivity with the last mile. If we remove our intellectually so-called 'vision' we will see the prosperity of the last decade in IT, Telecom, other sectors, and balance of payments, they have really affected only top 5-10 % of the population. The fundamentals at the bottom of the pyramid have not changed much. Though we have reasonable access to telephones and television sets, we have hardly made a dent in water, sanitation, primary education, health, housing, and eradication of disguised starvation. We have to remove our elitist sunglasses to see a more complete picture of reality.

9. Concentration

There are individuals who do not have concentrationon the job or target and as a result cannot deliver or achieve. Similarly there are organizations which are having split concentration. Without focus and concentration, no organisation can succeed or achieve excellence. We all know the famous story of the power of concentration of Arjun as in the *Mahabharata*.

Swami Vivekananda rightly said: "While you may be careful about what you pay for with your money, you are probably less careful about what you pay for your attention. In the long run, how you spend your attention affects your life far more profoundly than how you spend your money. Your attention is the strongest currency at your disposal."

Similarly this is true for any organization. Concentration / comprehension for any organization is a must particularly when the market is flooded with information, data & knowledge. As Alexander Solzhenitsyn rightly says: "Our capacity for concentration...being overwhelmed by a tidal wave of ordinate superficial information."

Swami Parthasarathy explained in the *'Vedanta Treaties'*: Concentration is defined as the intellect supervising the mind to remain in the present. The mind has to be continuously supervised as it travels back and forth-to the past and future-with equal velocity. An unleashed mind can cause self-destruction. An unwavering mind is the ultimate power of concentration.

To excel you need concentration, clarity, alertness, and a highly flexible balance of skills. You need a combination of a cool, steady mind and a high level of intellect and as Swami Vivekananda said: "Concentration is the essence of all knowledge; nothing can be done without it. Ninety percent of thought force is wasted by the ordinary human being......"

10. Create dreams

Like human beings, an organization to must have a dream. A dream has unlimited power to inspire. The organisation has to appreciate and respect that dream, for a dream motivates to put effort and take actions.

"The dreamers are the saviours of the world. As the visible world is sustained by the invisible, so men, throughout all their trials and troubles, are nourished by the beautiful vision of their dreamers. Cherish your visions, cherish your ideals. Cherish the music that stirs in your heart, the loveliness that drapes your purest thoughts. For out of these, if you but remain true to them your world will at last be built.

To desire is to obtain; to aspire is to achieve. Shall man's lowest desires receive the fullest gratification, and his purest aspirations starve for lack of sustenance? such is not the Law. Such a condition can never obtain: "Ask and receive."

Dream lofty dreams, and as you dream, so shall you become. Your vision is the promise of what you shall one day be. Your ideal is the prophecy of what you shall at last unveil. the greatest achievement was at first a dream. Your circumstances may be unhappy, but they shall not remain so if you perceive an ideal and strive to reach it. You can't travel within and and stand still without. In all human affairs there are efforts,and there are results. The strength of the effort is the measure of the result. Gifts, powers, material, intellectual, and spiritual possessions are the fruits of effort. They are thoughts completed, objectives accomplished, vision realised. The vision that you glorify in your mind, the ideal that you enthrone in your heart-this you will build your life by; this you will become."-says James Allen in *'As a Man Thin*keth'. This is quite relevant for any organisation as well as an individual.

11. Convert dreams into reality

To convert dreams into reality, we must be open to change, be willing to learn and unlearn, and above all, be fearless in facing challenges. 'Dreams get done when you are transparent with your intentions. 'Work with passion—not only core people are to be engaged with passion, but the whole organisation is required to be engaged.

A context to be created to eliminate employee mentality. Ownership mentality has to be developed. Only then dreams can be converted into reality. Effeciency productivity are the result of genuine interest. Some people produce no matter where they work because they are internally motivated. They like to complete what they set out to do. They think of a task as being meaningful in itself. However, the commitment to completion only goes so far with anyone.

Enjoyment is the key to any successful endeavour. To withstand the market forces, employees should start thinking like entrepreneurs, which means they have to act as if they own the business in which they work. Ownership mentality can be developed if the employees are engaged with the passion of socio-economic value creation. Focusing on value creation stimulates creativity and innovation since an ownership mindset motivates employees to come up with ways to do a better job for the society, which improves their overall problem-solving ability.

Converting dreams into reality depends on the context which facilitates the combination and summation of the following:

- People
- Passion
- Positiveness
- Principle
- Purpose
- Perseverance
- Pride

12. Change orientation

Change as the way of life has to be accepted. It is not sufficient to understand or comprehend reality but to accept change and strive to change the situation. Most of the variables in reality are beyond the control of any organisation (even the biggest corporation in the world); the organisation has to face continuous challenges of various kinds: political, competitor, government policy, technological, international situation, natural calamities and war etc. To face this, the organisation must have:

- Courage
- Confidence
- Can-do attitude
- Cohesive team spirit

Organisations have to be proactive and should ceaselessly reinvent themselves, their products, services, strategies and systems. For this they need scale, managerial competence and financial resources. But the most important factors: they need an ambitious, can-do leadership and high quality talent. Capital and technology are available in the market. The key factor which makes the difference is the leadership of the core team and employees who are inspired by core values to accept the challenges.

Change cannot be continuously achieved if it is only the brilliant ideas of a few. Ownership has to be established. Change can only be continuously pursued when employees across the board see the benefits of change and participate in the process.

13. Collective and Collaborative wisdom

Collective or collaborative approach is required to be adopted. Internal cooperation is very vital for any organisation to create value. Internal cooperation is a must among different departments, different levels of people and different layers in the organisation to use the human talent to its potential. The company should sincerely believe that CEOs cannot build the institution. Their charisma is no substitute for collective wisdom and cumulative knowledge of many people. Collective collaborative wisdom is always superior to individual brilliance.

Several companies have already started realising that there is no substitute for collective wisdom and started accepting team or collective leadership. By different methods or procedure it is being practised. But the percentage of companies is very few where collective leadership is being accepted and practised.

'Team character' is required to be developed to ensure the learning and utilisation of cumulative and collective knowledge wisdom. We have to come out from 'single-point' decision making where founder-promoters / CEOs are taking all decisions to 'circle-point' decision where collective wisdom is to be utilized and decisions are taken. Why collaborative character ? Collaborative character is the necessity for survival due to:

- Business issues / problems are very complex.
- No individual, single discipline / function can give the solution. Integration / co-opertaion of all functions and activities are required to be appreciated.
- Response time can be reduced since data / information is shared and discussed.
- Implementation becomes easy since ownership of the problem and decision are shared by the team.
- Conscience and core values are kept.
- Acts as checks and balance. This approach can ensure that organisational interest is first and not the egos of individuals.

A team of CEOs is required for decision-making and they should genuinely believe in creative collaboration. Azim Premji, Chairman, Wipro Ltd. rightly said: "The challenges ahead are so complex that no individual will be able to face them alone. While most of our education is focussed on individual streangth, teaming with others is equally important. You cannot fire a missile from a canoe. Unless you build a strong network of people with complimentary skills, you will be restricted by your own limitations."

At all levels of the company, a cohesive team is required. Fundamentals of cohesive TEAM are:

- T: Target to achieve.
- E: Effort to balance ego
- A: Attitude to adjust
- M: Motivation to contribute.

To build an institution everybody should believe that the secret of success' is the TEAM. Even with technological innovations, the human spirit still remains the biggest asset, and team work , the best support system. Evey member of the team can make a difference—understanding, communication and dialogue are the foundations. People should believe that it is a reward, a challenge and a privilege to be a contributing member of a TEAM. As Bob Woolmer, a cricket coach rightly defined the meaning of TEAM : Together Everyone Achieves More.

In one of the internet messages, the essence and significance of 'team' was explained beautifully, which all organisations as well as individuals should try to follow:

In the fall when you see geese heading south for the winter flying along in the "V" formation, you might be interested in knowing what science has discovered about why they fly that way. It has been learned that as each bird flaps its wings, it creates uplift for the bird immediately following. By flying in a "V" formation, the whole flock adds at least 71% greater flying range than if each bird flew on its own.

- *The lesson is: People who are part of a team and share a common direction get where they are going quicker and easier, because they are traveling on the trust of one another and lift each other up along the way.*

Whenever a goose falls out of formation, it suddenly feels the drag and resistance of trying to go through it alone and quickly gets back into formation to take advantage of the power of the flock.

- *The lesson is : If we have as much sense as a goose, we will stay in formation and share information with those who are heading the same way that we are going.*

When the lead goose gets tired, he rotates back in the wing and another goose takes over.

- *The lesson is : It pays to share leadership and take turns doing hard jobs*

The geese honk from behind to encourage those upfront to keep up their speed.

- *The lesson is : Words of support and inspiration help energize those on the front line, helping them to keep pace in spite of the day-to-day pressures and fatigue. it is important that our honking be encouraging, other wise it's just-well-honking!*

Finally, when a goose gets sick or is wounded by a gunshot and falls out, two geese fall out of the formation and follow the injured one down to help and protect him. They stay with him until he is either able to fly or until he is dead, and then they launch out with another formation to catch up with their group.

- *The lesson is : When one of us is down, it's upto others to stand by us in our time of trouble. If we have the sense of a goose, we will stand by each other when things get rough. We will stay in formation with those headed where we want to go.*

Swami Tejomayananda explained the essence of Team:".. When organisations fail, for instance, it is because of lack of co-operation and understanding among the members; there is no team spirit. The spirit of Yajna involves giving up our ego and selfishness, our sense of "I" and "mine" and endeavour to grow through joint efforts".

14. Complacence

Several companies failed or underperformed due to complacency. For continuous improvement and achievement of excellent performance the organization should be guided by latent fear "......Fear should guide you, but it should be latent, I consider the prospect of failure on regular basis. " says Bill Gates, Chief Software Architect, Microsoft.

At a time when unpredictable winds of change are blowing stronger than before,companies irrespective of their size are often caught between remaining as silent spectators in the technology race due to sheer complacency enabling competitors to gain the competitive edge, or plunging into high technology investment without knowing the stakes and rules of the competition. We need an open mind to look at things in a different way and allow new inputs to come in. Otherwise, there is real danger of becoming complacent or downright arrogant. Pranesh Misra rightly mentioned in a recent article:

"Civilisations, kingdoms, countries, stocks...all go through a cyclical phase of success and failure. Failure follows success, because success breeds an implicit faith in the past and that becomes the main pillar of failure. Complacency, laziness and arrogance are the other pillars of failure that success breeds."

15. Clear sense of direction

The world is becoming turbulent and organizations are becoming resilient. Strategic resilience is not about responding to a one-time crisis. It's not about rebounding from a setback. It's about continuously anticipating and adjusting to deep, secular trends that can permanently impair the earning capacity of a core business. It's about having the capacity to change before the case for change becomes desperately obvious.

Achieving strategic resilience is not easy. Any company that can make sense of its environment, can generate strategic options and realign its resources faster than its rivals and will enjoy cutting edge. Without a clear sense of direction this is not possible.

16. Consultation

Context or atmosphere to be created for genuine consultation within the organisation. There should be a process for dialogue consultation not debate. We should differentiate between debate and dialogue. Dialogue is not shouting or using diplomatic words or confusing the issue deliberately or hiding one's ignorance, neither is it giving lecture in colleges or seminars.

Dialogues require a genuine participative culture that motivates and facilitates listening to other viewpoints with respect and takes positive approach to learn and accept for improvement. In a debate people are compelled to oppose others point of view to prove own superiority and to dominate the situation. The skill to manage consultation effectively and to arrive at decisions is the key.

For value creation genuine dialogue is crucial and is the most critical approach. Context is to be reated where people can have dialogue, consultation, discover and plan the best course of action for dealing with complex situations. Core people must never be shy of dialogue consultation and must listen carefully to what their people want to say. People should be confident and comfortable to participate in the process of consultation or dialogue.

17. Concern for value creation

Organisations should not focus on making money; on the other hand focus should be to understand value addition matrix and to decide & scale the level of value addition given the constraint. Understanding the value matrix is extremely important.

Matter cannot be created or destroyed. This is the theory of conservation of matter. "Nothing is lost in the universe. Matter turns into energy, energy turns into matter" says Buddha. We are only changing the form by various socio-economic activities which is called value creation. Any product or service is nothing but change of form. In value creation both physical and mental labour is involved. Mental labour is always a dominant factor in value creation. The Society, country or world will be dominated by those organizations who are trying to offer product / services where percentage of mental contribution is much more than physical labour / activities.

One of the important social contradictions is between physical and mental labour. A scientist, engineer, MBA or consultant is getting much more remuneration than an agricultural or industrial labour. This is universally true all over the world. A balancesheet company cannot be transformed into a great institution without understanding the importance of the higher level of value creation in terms of society and the customer point of view. This is not possible without sincere concern for customer and society. This is true for individuals, society, economic organization as well as the country.

If you see any developed country and a poor country the difference is in contribution of mental labour in value creation. If you take any great organization or institution this is also universally true.

Yves Doz is a world-renowned Professor at INSEAD, France argues that there are three layers of value someone can create or add, and each of these three requires a different mindset.

1. The Adaptive layer
2. The experiential layer
3. The existential layer

1. The adaptive layer

The lowest layer of value addition / creation is technical, like supplying of raw materials including manpower.

2. The experiential layer

You do not play on your ability to intermediate between the access to raw material and the end user of it. You 'step into the shoes' of the customer,and create valuable products and services. It is about stepping into the shoes of the customer to experientially feel the need.

3. The existential layer

They not only know how to get into the shoes of the customer, but as Doz says, "they creep into the mind of the customer" and work backward from there to create products and services.

Great service approach or mind-set

We have to also understand the 'great service' mentality. Good service is problem solving-delivering what people expect to receive. Great service is getting below the surface of the problem-delivering what no one expects to receive. It's listening, learning, assessing, refining our approach to deliver solution. Great service requires sound judgement and good judgement starts with knowledge / intelligence with insight and creative expression. The result is a permament conversation / dialogue about quality, performance, standard and value addition.

Any company wanting to become an institution has to combine:

- Existential layer approach
- Great service approach

Great institutions should focus on 'socio-economic value' creation instead of superficial value addition.

Wealth Added Index not relevant

Lot of equations / models are available to measure the wealth or value creation by the companies mainly based on stock market expectation or rate of change of expectation. For example : Wealth added=Change in Market Capitalisation-Required Return+Dividends-New Equity Issues. The Wealth Added Index basically reflects what investors expect of their companies and how much the management is actually delivering. This is shareholder value- driven approach. Concern for customer, society & country is not in the picture at all.

If a company exists for customers, then where is the customer in the matrix? This is not intrinsic value, merely a speculative value with nothing to do with customer value. If we really want to transform a balancesheet company into an institution, socio-economic value matrix has to be formulated otherwise we will be fooled by some clever manipulator and by some manipulative accounting and statistical jargon without any substance.

Basics of value creation

Organisation must have the sincerity and commitment for socio-economic value creation and understand the basics of value creation:

1. **Customer value :**
   - In terms of experience of quality, price, convenience information
2. **Social value:**
   - Contribution for new job opportunities whether direct/indirect
   - Inspiration / confidence

- Affordability by the low income people-to bring them in the market network.
- Contribution to improve the standard of living of the vast majority of population
- Social trust

3. Economic value:

- Capital-Output ratio
- New technology introduction
- Utilisation of surplus fund –capital allocation model
- Contribution in percentage of GDP
- Contribution in export

4. Environmental value:

- Contribution to maintain environment and ecological balance

18. Constant & Open communication channels

Communication should become the unifying cord of the organization mind, the individual employee and the external world. It should reflect the letters and spirit of the organisation mind. The inner strength , dynamism and enthusiasms of the corporate mind should truly be reflected.

Communication channels should be open in the true sense as suggested by George Heilmeire, Chairman Emeritus, Bellcore: "The CEO needs to be open to dialogue and have his people see that he is not sitting in a hierarchical mode with respect to the company. He must demonstrate that he is creating an open organization and is willing to share information and build the free exchange of ideas."

Zig Zigler's prescription in the context of selling is also quite relevant : "Remain in close communication with the field-force and listen to what they have to say. In the world of selling, if the manager does not listen to the salesperson and their experience of what's happening out there, then he begins to lose touch with the reality of today and the reality of today determines how good the business is going to be tomorrow."

19. Creating caring context

To make a great organization / institution we have to understand the fact that employees perform best when they feel comfortable with the work environment. For employees to attain their full potential, it is essential for the organization to make them feel cared for, to nurture their talent and creativity and inspire them constantly as they go about their tasks. It is not enough for companies to have managers who focus on merely achieving the organisation's goals, rather, they must have leaders who can inspire, motivate, guide and drive their teams to ever-greater accomplishments and thereby create a great institution.

20. Concern for details

We are generally comfortable with the big picture in making strategy, policy planning. But business ultimately depends on execution of the plan and 75% of our work is just doing the detailing and specifically the micro-detailing. Without detailing excellent execution is impossible. "Strategy equals execution. All the great ideas and visions in the world are worthless if they cannot be implemented rapidly and efficiently." says Colin Powell.

If any organisation really wants to be connected with the reality, it has to understand the significance of detailing as

Donald Trump puts it:... "No matter how accomplished you are, no matter how well you think you know your business, you have to remain vigilant about the details of your field. You can't get by on experience or smarts. Even the best surgeons need to be retrained regularly, to stay current on the latest research. No matter what you are managing, don't assume you can glide by, momentum is something you have to work at to maintain."

21. Cultivate inspiration as capital

"Inspiration is needed in geometry, just as much in poetry" says Aleksandr Sergeyvich Pushkin.

Inspiration is one of the motivating forces for socio-economic activity. Great human endeavours are guided by inspiration. Mahatma Gandhi, Netaji, Swami Vivekananda, Ramakrishna, Gautam Buddha who transformed the social consciousness of millions of people and inspired them to take the initiative and sacrifice for social-economic emancipation of millions of others. All these people did not have any physical capital, and even then they made great contributions for mankind only by inspiration.

We have to understand the latent power of inspiration, which no physical asset can match. This has unlimited power. If you leap through the human history all social, economic, political, scientific and technological transformation have taken place because of inspiration, and not because of dead assets.

Our freedom struggle, the Long March of China, the Russian Revolution, freedom of America, the transformation of Japan into an economic powerhouse-all revolutionary events are based on inspiration.

If a balancesheet company wants to become a great institution, inspiration has to be considered as capital;

cultivated and nurtured. People are required to become engaged by 'inspiration.'

Organisational context is required to be open and transparent for inspiration to flourish and which is true for individuals also. Jan Gordon rightly observed:"...Being inspired requires an openness of heart and spirit. Create an environment that supports an open heart, so that inspiration blossoms in your life. Just as a flower needs soil and water, so too does inspiration need openness of heart and spirit. Inspiration can't exist without this."

22. Competence

Holding people hostage to 'core competence' restricts them. Potential is to be respected and tapped. It is more productive to create competences around people and processes to create value. This promotes flexibility, encourages growth and the value add-on will far exceed anything a conventional approach can bring.

'Core competence' limits the thinking and creative ability of the people. Competence which is to be developed for value creation should not be prisoner of particular activities or a particular line of business. There are several companies which have entered completely different areas and achieved excellence. In the ultimate analysis the determination, creativity, imagination, effort and courageous patience decides the outcome.

This is true for individuals also. Without any background people have taken the challenge and established a successful company. Bill Gates, a college drop-out, created the most powerful company in the world-what was his core competence? We should not reduce the human mind to a conformist vacuity. Organisation should unshackle people's innate and spontaneous intelligence and channelise it for value creation.

23. Concern for people

Businesses are about people. Revenues come from the efforts of the people. Growth comes from customer appreciation and acceptance. Again people. Costs are borne on people. No business can exist on the basis of models, data or the so-called consultants' projections, estimates and theories. Most of these projections, estimates and recommendations do not conform to the dynamics of the market realities. These are too off the mark.

Understanding the integration and differentiation of people, and utilizing their people is the key for building an institution, and not the data, model, theory or consultants' complicated model or statistical estimate.

It is to be understood that money may earn a person's presence, it does not earn their passion. A 'People first' context has to be created. All HR-related issues are to be aligned in that direction. Organisation should focus on :

- Transparency, trust and openness
- Feeling of being wanted—company is thinking about them and values them
- Informal atmosphere free of politics
- Core values—thics, fairness, kindness, efficiency, effectiveness and exceptional customer concern.
- Spirit of entrpreneurship or ownership
- Flexibility, freedom and encouragement to make decisions
- Context inspires people with a sense that work is valuable and worth doing.

- Keep HR fundamentals simple without hype and superficial jargon.

For commitment or concern to people, we should learn from the Japanese model or atleast accept the Japanese approach as a reference. In Japan they really believe organisation means 'people'. They consider an organisation as a collection of people. Each employee is considered as a contributing member of the organisation. The individual employee is utilized to the fullest extent of his or her creative and productive capacity through various programmes and participative schemes like suggestion schemes,quality circle, TQM, value engineering etc. "Tell me and I'll forget ; show me and I may remember ; involve me and I will understand."- lesson from this Chinese proverb is quite relevant to unleash the potential of the people.

Japanese company starts with people, or individual constituents, trusting their capabilities and potential. The whole organisation looks organic and entrepreneurial, as opposed to the mechanistic and bureaucratic of western model. It is less planned, less rigid, but more vision or mission-driven.

24. Consider human talent as capital

Human beings should be considered as capital and not as resource. Resource is always limited and cannot be stretched whereas the capability of a human being is unlimited. This distinction is to be understood in the true sense. Different aspects of human talent are required to be creatively synthesized and synergised:

Human Talent Parameters	**Attributes**
Intellectual	• Intelligence • Inventive creativity • Knowledge and knowledge for information management • Domain skills • Completence • Anlytical ability
Social	• Net-working capability • Relationship management • Capability for social innovations
Attitude	• Commitment • Determination • Confidence • Ability to face-challenges • Ability to take risk • Ability to think beyond core competence
Emotional	• Propensity to lead • Ambition • Initiative • Belief in core values

Transformation of the organisation depends on the right convergence, synthesis and leverage of all the aspects of human talent. This is possible if the 'context' is conducive and that again depends on the right corporate character.

In most of the cases, human talent is not being utilised properly. How many of our large corporations are really interested in projects outside current business activities? They focus only on balancesheet numbers. In most of the companies, there is no long term strategy for innovation and creative application of technology and process.

New technology does not come on a chip, it comes from people's mind and R&D effort. Proper investment in people and R&D is a critical parameter. Core focus should be on developing new intellectual property and patents which can be utilised for offering better product or services for the benefit of society and country. Most of the companies are allocating very little funds for reaserch and development. India's performance is dismal in patent and intellectual property.

People have started realising that human talent is a kind of 'last frontiers' for competitive advantage since it is observed in reality that new technology, upgraded processes, marketing strategy or financial strategy can only provide limited opportunity and differentiation in the market place. Not superficial differentiation, but real differentiation is the key in the marketplace to get competitive advantage which can be achieved only through effective and creative utilisation of the human talent.

"Power in the knowledge economy resides more with knowledge workers than with the owners or managers. Serving the needs of those workers is a new leadership imperative. Research shows not only the characteristics of effective leaders but also the expectations that followers have of their leaders."- says Warren Bennis, Leadership expert.

25. Concept of feudalism

Though formal feudalism was abolished long back, but the mindset still persists and has not changed. The king does not do any mistake i.e Promoters / CEOs cannot do any mistake. No unquestionable can be questioned. Promoter's sons / daughters are naturally born talented like kings / queens and can become CEOs without any test. Shobhaa De, has in a one of per article observed : "We claimed to have shed old hierarchies and inhibitions, regarding caste, community and social status. But have we? Most affluent people, even in this day and age,treat their domestics like lowly chattels. Most industrialists suffer from a feudalistic *'maalik-naukar'* mindset that stops them from accepting even top professionals as colleagues."

This mentality has to be eliminated. Only contribution and merit should be the criteria. Ideas are no one's monopoly. There is no equitable distribution of knowledge, expertise and energy. This has to be sincerely appreciated and practised.

26. Concern for quality

Quality should be ingrained in the corporate character; otherwise only lip service will be given; the ground reality in most of the companies. In most of the cases the core group is not much concerned about the quality issues. It is generally left to the quality department and down the line managers who are again concerned about the production target. Most of the top people are worried about:

- Quality and cost trade-off
- Quality and production trade-off
- Quality and profit trade-off

Several procedures / jargons are introduced either to impress outsiders or for image building exercise; but do not have much involvement from the core group, or there is no genuine interest to implement and practice in true sense.

There are several quality tools which are being practised or introduced but still the quality scene is very pathetic in reality. Some of the tools or concepts are:

- Zero defect
- Quality circle

- TQM
- ISO 9000
- Six Sigma
- Customer Satisfaction Measurement

All these ultimately become fads and are eventually replaced by another fads. Even there is a lot of debate about the interpretation of these theories to determine which one is better than the other. Most of the time managers are totally confused. An example of the so-called 'difference' between TQM and SIX Sigma:

TQM	SIX SIGMA
It is about the business of quality	It is about the quality of business
It is philosophical, prophetic in nature	It is a goal-oriented, result-oriented, fact-based system of management. Repeatable management process based on the idea of measurement.

This is just an example to show that even the most informed and knowledgeable manager will also be totally confused. Dr. Joseph Juran, a living legend in quality movements, rightly observed:" Six Sigma is just a new name for old quality. It will quickly go the way of the other fads, like re-engineering."

Quality has to be part of core values and the core group has to be part of it otherwise all other efforts will be just lip srvice without much significance. Commitment to quality is a must. As Mark H. McCormack stated: "I cannot think of any business where such commitment does not apply. Start with the best, or what you think is going to be the best. It will get you started on the right foot; it's the only absolute competitive edge; and it's like working with a net : a hedge that will minimize bad decisions and maximize good ones in the future."

27. Cultivate action orientation

Organisation should eliminate the 'thinking, planning and talking syndrome'. Effectiveness of any idea, plan, strategy & programme ultimately depends on implementation and implemetation depends on concrete / specific actions or series of actions to be taken. For actions, comprehensive detailing is required to be done and step-by-step or part-by-part actions to be taken. This is called the delivery system which is requred to be monitored, reviewed, modified and directed on day-to-day basis to achieve the result as per planning. The execution or implementation burden has to be owned. Thomas Henry Huxley rightly observed: "The great end of life is not knowledge but action."

In most of the cases we believe in discussion, debating, plan preparation, presentation but when it comes to take the rigorous burden of detailing the implementation we suffer from intellectual intertia and try to pass the responsibility to others. Organisation must create a context for outstanding execution. Execution is the key—both in quality and speed—as Morpheus said in *The Matrix*: "There's a difference between knowing the path,and walking the path."

There are people who are very good, articulate and can make a sophisticated powerpoint presentation, create impression by putting jargons or theories but are very ineffective in implementing on the ground because they are not ready to take the challenge to bring progress or real change by actions.

In reality we are only solving the problem or giving better solutions to old problems. No problem can be solved without action-thought, idea, plan and decision will remain on paper only. In personal life, in the organisation's context and the nation's context- this is universally true. "The world is the field of action. Through action one acquire knowledge" says Sri Ramakrishna Paramahansa.

Decision, discussion, debate, and analysis are necessary conditions but not sufficient to move forward, to bring changes and improvements or solve the problem faced by any company. *In 'Ten Deadly Sins'* Kotler had lamented that companies are failing not because of theory but because of practice, implementation or action.

Context has to be created where action / practice or implementation is encouraged and rewarded and the discussion, debate, presentation syndrome' is discouraged. Colin Powell rightly said: "Strategy equals execution. All the great ideas and visions in the world are worthless if they can't be implemented rapidly and efficiently."

For effective execution or implementation following are required to be ensured:

- Ownership of decision, plan or strategy.
- Collaborative effort
- Focus or rewards for action / implementation
- Discourage superficial discussion, debate, meeting and presentation
- Unconditional commitment to achieve the milestones

We have to genuinely appreciate that the world is not understood by contemplation but by action. 'The hand is the cutting edge of the mind.'

Kenichi Ohmae wrote in his book, *'Mind of the Strategist'* : "Corporate performance is the result of combining planning and execution. It resembles a boat race. No matter how hard each crew member rows, if the coxswain does not choose the right direction, the crew can never hope to win. Conversely,even if the coxswain is a perfect navigator, you cannot win the race unless the rowers strive hard in unison."

28. Concern for equilibrium/unity

"The beginning of thought is in disagreement—not only with others but also with ourselves." -says Eric Hoffer, Karl Marx stated in his famous theory 'dialectical materialism' that matter exists because of unity of opposites. Even the atom- the minutest particle of matter—has the unity of opposites. In society also there is contradiction and at the same time there is unity. India is the best example of unity in diversity or contradiction. We cannot expect there would be uniformity in language, food, culture, social practices, habits or religions. But the whole country is bound / united by the feeling of the motherland—Bharat. This feeling is the binding cord.

Any organisation has several internal contradictions:

- Contradiction in the board.
- Contradiction in top management
- Contradiction between departments
- Contradiction between employees and management
- Contradiction among the employees

Nobody should think there should be unity in perceptions, understanding approach. There have to be differences. That is the natural rule. Uniformity is unnatural. However, equilibrium has to be achieved through the core values. Core values should become the binding / unifying factor. No other factor can be substitute of core values. An organisation should genuinely accept that contradiction is the dynamic force. It has to be channelised in a positive direction to get the synergy. This can only be done through unity of core values. This is the equilibrium of opposite forces. Steven R.Covey observes : "The new ideal is the complementary team where unity is achieved by people who have different talents-who have one vision and purpose but many roles, perceptions, capacities, and duties."

Nature is the best example of harmony in diversity. Air, water, trees, forest, animals, seasons, land, rivers, sun, moon, stars—all are having differences and diversities in the universe but they are all in harmony or in equilibrium. This diversity and equilibrium is inherent for the existence of the universe. In organisation also context is to be created to follow: Tolerate the cacophony before you find the harmony.'

29. Consistency

Organisation should not be run or managed by whims and fancies of the promoters or top management. Consistency means organisation must have the context and approach to avoid erratic, rigid, bureaucratic, mechanistic and adhoc way of functioning.

Organisation must be consistent towards the core values in spirit and action. All activities should be guided by core values.Employees and all other stakeholders should be treated responsibly and consistently not arbitarily. Organisations should maintain consistency in their attitude and approach to employees, customers, suppliers and business partners.

Consistency basically means core values or purposes will remain unaltered while business strategy, tactics and practices endlessly adapt to changing environment or market situation. Inconsistency in approach leads to all sorts of unnecessary tensions and anxieties in people as well as other stake holders.

Another basic aspect is that organisation should be consistently flexible—that it is going beyond the status quo to adopt to new realities. Consistent flexibility has to be in-built in the organisation's approach. People should perceive that flexibility. Few years back, most of the companies used to spend lot of time and effort for long term & strategic planning, but today it is extremely critical and important to build a high degree of flexibility into such plans so that they may be adopted quickly to changes in the market and socio-economic areas. Flexibility means constant review and evaluation of the opportunities or alternatives available and the cost and benefit to respond creatively and innovatively to the changes in the environment and the situation the organisation is facing. For continuous socio-economic value creation, the organisation has to cultivate and appreciate continuity, coherence and congruence of approach.

30. Comfort for failure

There has to be a sense of comfort for failure. Context has to be created for acceptance of failure. Without celebrating failure success cannot be achieved or goal cannot be achieved. People will be too scared to take the initiative. People will be discouraged to take a decision. People will be demotivated for creativity or innovation. 'Failure is the mother of success. 'This spirit has to be respected and encouraged. If there is no positiveness in 'failure', then how can it be considered as the mother of success?

Failure and success can be seen as two sides of the same coin. Failure provides valuable real-life lessons that can build the foundations for future success. In the language of Rabindranath Tagore : "When we watch a child trying to walk, we see its countless failures ; its successes are but few. If we had to limit our observation within a narrow space of time, the sight would be cruel." The first step of all creativity or innovation or discovery is the acceptance of failure. Failure has to be appreciated for:

- To unlock the full potential of individual
- To encourage innovation/creativity
- Commitment to question status quo and continuous value creation

Winston Churchill rightly advised: "Success is the ability to go from failure to failure without losing your enthusiasm."

When Thomas Edison was working on the light bulb he had one failure after another during the process. He said to the critics who commented about all the times it appeared he had failed with his invention: "I've simply eliminated twenty—seven ways that don't work." Organisation must accept that breakdowns can lead to breakthroughs.

31. Constructive dissent

It is the easiest thing to follow the crowd, agree with boss, collegues, general opinion and 'fit in the groove'. The most common mindset is to accept the status quo without questioning. Organisation has to respect and encourage constructive dissent or different points of view and discourage the hypocrite, sycophant and conformist mind. Also the habitual dissenter should not take advantage of the openness of the company.

The organisation should sincerely believe that it's most important asset is its collection of employees having their own minds which can challenge the status quo and make the valuable contribution for value creation. Most of the world's innovations, and discoveries took place due to questioning the status quo or seeing the things through different eyes. Different points of view or dissent will be constructive if the following are ensured:

- Discourage dissent for the sake of dissent
- Keeping in mind the core values
- Determination to implement the idea
- Dissent with responsibility
- Dissent with creativity or innovation
- Purpose to contribute for value creation

Continuous encouragement to challenge the status quo is required. We should not be satisfied with the status quo. We should sincerely believe that continuous learning and improvement are the most critical aspects for value creation in a continuous manner.

The spirit of dissent is captured by a statement of Thomas Watson, Jr., Former Chief Executive, IBM :" I never hesitated to promote some one I did not like. The comfortable assistant, the nice guy you like to go on fishing trips with, is a great pitfall. Instead, I looked for those sharp, scratchy, harsh, almost unpleasant guys who see and tell you about things as they really are. If you can get enough of them around you and have patience enough to hear them out,there is no limit to where you can go."

32. Consider 'time' as input

'Time' is one of the most important inputs. Most of the organisations ignore it or do not understand the implication of time in terms of value creation, since this is invisible and not exactly quantifiable. Moreover, till date there is no attempt to factor in 'time' as an input in profit and loss calculation.

Time is an invisible contributor for value creation is true for individuals, organisations, customers as well as the society at large. Effectiveness of any individual to a great extend depends on how creatively or purposefully time is utilised.

Similarly this is true for an organisation also. Any organisation wants to create value, it has to understand the importance of the time factor in relation to the organisation's competitiveness, efficiency and effectiveness as well as the customer comfort and convenience.

When change accelerates, the ability to squeeze time-for instance, by communicating swiftly, executing project in a rapid speed or bringing new product or services to market fast can be- the ultimate cutting edge. The critical issue is how whole organisation has to align to understand the importance of the time input in relation to the following::

- To gather /collect information /data / knowledge
- To analyse and distribute information / data / knowledge
- To aquire knowledge to apply knowledge creatively/ innovatively
- To make decision or formulate business model
- To execute/implement business model / project
- To recruit effective people
- To reduce production time or process
- To provide service at higher speed
- To reduce time in supply chain linkages
- To respond to environmental changes including competition.

If we analyse the evaluation of products and services from the stone age to modern age, one of the important aspects of value creation is the reduction of the time element. For example:

- Stone equipments to modern computer controlled machine/robot or automation system.

- Plough to mechanised tiller.
- Hand writing to Type writer to PC.
- Bullock cart to super car to supersonic jet.
- Post card to telephone/FAX to internet.
- Carbon copy to xerox to scanner.
- Raw food to ready-made cooked food.
- Physical market to E-market
- Physical meeting and discussion to video-meeting and discussion.

Organisations have to aquire knowledge to creatively use the time input to create value which makes the real difference.

2. Corporate Personality

It is a reflection of the overall corporate character. Without personality, character cannot be expressed and communicated. This is true for an individual as well as an organisation. Corporate personality is important to build credibility and authenticity. Personality is expressed or reflected by various activities, communication process - annual report, magazine, news bulletin, symbols logo, slogan, office get up, core people's behaviour, employees' average behaviour, social-interaction, PR exercise etc.

Corporate personality is the expression or reflection of the consolidated form of core values and basic characters perceived by the employees and other stakeholders like customers, suppliers, investors, civic community and even the political establishment. Inshort, personality basically reflects concerns, convictions and character of the organisation.

Personality is an asset. Personality is important to connect the core values with the employees and build trust and credibility with the external environment. In India some of the companies have already built that personality like Tata, HDFC, Infosys, Wipro, Amul. These names express or communicate trust, transparency, sophistication, quality etc.

Personality is the resultant effect of various factors. However, organisation has to take concrete action to build this. Personality brings a huge impact in relating to the employees, customers and society to get their trust, loyalty and confidence. Corporate personality should reflect genuineness of purpose and values of the company which is possible if the following are adhered to:

- Avoid phoniness / cunningness
- Avoid superficiality
- Consistent with core values, slogans and actions
- Maintain integrity in communication

Symbols and slogans play a vital role in facilitating the creation of personality. Till date 'Bande Mataram', even after so many years is the most powerful slogan and song which ignites feelings of nationalism, patriotism and unity of the nation.

'Ma Durga' having ten hands and accompanied by other gods and goddesses symbolises the personality which expresses power and resource to destroy evil and protect innocents and also the eternal truth. Society can easily relate to that.

Army uniform, bearing, presentation of army personnel express personality of the tough, strong and smart which citizens can trust for protection of the country.

Netaji Subhas Chandra Bose's, personality expressed: heroism, freedom, sacrifice, dedication, nationalism. His historical call to his countrymen : "Give me blood, I will give you freedom" really inspired and motivated millions of people to fight and sacrifice for the motherland.

Gandhiji's personality expressed: simplicity, peace, harmony, emancipation, honesty, non-violence, mass leadership, social good, freedom and he could motivate, and mobilise millions of people during the freedom struggle.

Swami Vivekananda's personality expressed youthfulness, humanity, courage, social good, universal brotherhood which still inspires millions of people.

Jesus Christ expressed forgiveness, peace, non-violence, sacrifice, universal brotherhood, emancipation of human beings which inspires millions of people even today.

Similarly, if any organisation wants to become an institution it has to build a personality so that it can inspire own employees and connect also with the other stakeholders and society at large.

There are several so-called big companies as per balancesheet numbers but have the personality of 'Bania' or 'Manipulator'. So not many have trust in them. Most of the public sector companies are having personalities of the bureaucratic, corrupt, inefficient. That's why they are not able to inspire their own employees and society at large." A product or a person is as good or as bad as the image conveyed by it / him....." wrote V B N Ram in an article *'The Image Is The Man,Mind your Image*.

3. Core Group Alignment

Core values/purpose will be on paper only unless the core group is sincere about the following:

- Honest about motives, means and ends.
- Honest in the pursuit of social good.
- Sincere in creative collaboration—united in their minds and united in their purpose.

- Should create context that encourages or discourages certain kinds of activities.
- Believes and owns the core values / purpose.

Without an alignment of the core group with core values /purpose and facilitation to transform the character nothing can be achieved, as Art Klenir, Organizational Learning consultant stated : "the primary purpose of an organisation is not, as many believe, to meet customer's needs, foster innovation or make a better world. Rather, organisations are set up, first and foremost, to fulfil the perceived desires and priorities of a 'core group' of people. As such, the success or failure of an organisation is determined by the behaviour of this key set of individuals."

Leadership of the core group

Transformation of the mind or liberation of Corporate Character are not possible without the sincerity of the top management / promoters. Instead of CEO it should be called CCF-Chief Character Facilitator or Chief Encouragement Officer. Role of CEO should be to transform the organisational mind and to create the context. The core team should align with the core values and create context to transform the character of the company.

In order to transform the corporate character, management must be sincere to get the right feedback. The top management should create context by introducing:

- Corporate character evaluation guide.
- Socio-economic value creation evaluation guide
- Follow up action in earnest

Several organisations are struggling to retain few people by introducing several schemes, procedures / and incentives etc. But they are missing the larger picture. Lot of employees will not be able to quit due to employment situation and will continuously underperform or give 'satisfactory underperformance.'

Creativity, ideas or innovation are the life blood of any organization. This cannot be achieved without the redistribution of knowledge / information among all employees. Colin Powell observed:" In a brain-based economy, your best assets are people...........Too often, people are assumed to be empty chess pieces to be moved around by grand viziers, which may explain why so many top managers immerse their calender time in deal making, restructuring and the latest management fads. How many immerse themselves in the goal of creating an environment where the best, the brightest,the most creative are attracted, retained and, most importantly, unleashed?"

Leadership should try to facilitate the creative voice of the team members and encourage team members to listen to one another in order to build a context that promotes and facilitates team work and inspired problem solving. It is to be ensured that context encourages flow of creativity and problem solving rather than concentrating on the problem Achieving goals requires the cooperation and collaboration of different people at different levels, hence it is absolutely essential to foster a team approach. Context has to be created in which people are comfortable to discuss, debate, discover and plan the best course of action for dealing with any issues, challenges or situations. Rosabeth Moss Kanter, Professor, Harvard Business School rightly observed in a recent interview: "So leadership certainly matters, but a leader does not create the performance alone. A leader may initiate the conditions for higher performance like a great coach does. But the great coach isn't in the field, it is all the players. So I would say what a leader does is create the condition and deliver confidence."

Leadership role should be in terms of the Chief Encouragement Officer rather than the Chief Egotistic Officer as Henry Mintzberg wrote : "Mostly leadership is about getting other people to be heroic in a sense.But what we have instead, are an increasing number of ego trips-leaders who are less concerned with stimulating others, and more with making big dramatic decisions themselves."

The quality of corporate character has to be ensured by the CEO / top management. They should function as Chief Facilitators of corporate character so that they can motivate others to play the role of socio-economic value creators. Quality of management is the key variable in determining the effectiveness. Managerial quality is not a question of merely professional competence but also of the strength of character and the depth of commitment. "The subject of integrity in an organisation is usually limited to poster or an internet download from the HR or the legal department. There is the occasional talk by a roving minion. In very few,top management stands up and talks about integrity..............organisational intent is clarified in moments of darkness.Only a breach shows how far an organisation will go to make a choice between what is right and what is convenient.......The most critical aspects of dealing with issues of integrity is the price a management is willing to pay.......,"says Subroto Bagchi in a recent article.

Any organisation which is not focussing on integrity has to pay a heavy price at some point or the other. The core group of the organisation must bring integrity to the core values. Core group must create communication channels to inspire all employees and other stakeholders to raise concerns related to probable or actual deviations from integrity standards-especially those that could damage the reputation of the organisation.All such channels and practices should be made integral parts of the corporate character.

Character cannot be quantified by a statistical model but some kind of directional approach can be established. In practice some kind of corporate character evaluation guide is required to be developed / formulated. There cannot be any hard and fast rule for evaluation. Practical aspects depend on the core people. An idea is given for the evaluation guide as ready reference:

02 points scale has been considered where CF - Completely Followed PF-Partly Followed and NF-Not Followed. CF-02,PF-01 and NF-0.

Figure 3.4: Corporate character evaluation guide

Parameters	CF	PF	NF
Core values	02	-	-
Concern for ethics / integrity	-	-	
Cultivate excellence	-	-	
Creativity / innovation	-	01	
Commitment	-	-	
Channeling intellectual diversity	-	-	
Concern for market / Society	-	-	
Concentration	-	-	-
Create dreams	-	-	-
Convert dreams into reality	-	-	
Change orientation	-	-	
Collective & collaborative wisdom	-	-	
Complacence	-	-	-
Clear sense of direction	-	-	
Consultation	-	-	-
Concern for value creation	-	-	-
etc	-	-	-

This is to be genuinely monitored and reviewed by the core team and corrective actions to be taken as required. The core team should really become the facilitator as the Wrren Bennis, Leadership Expert, stated lucidly "Exemplary leaders believe they have a responsibility to extend people's growth. And to create an environment where people constantly learn. Those are the surest ways to generate intellectual capital and to use that capital to create new value. In the next century, that will be every leader's ultimate task."

Leadership should also understand that there is a difference between a constructive leader and creative leader. Constructive leader is happy with the status quo or very efficient in maintaining the existing business. Constructive leader is tradition-bound, averse to change, unimaginative and lacks critical sense. Creative leader creates a new world, new hope, new dream, new vision,new opportunity, new value. Creative leader believes in freedom to debate, dialogue, freedom to explore ideas and tolerate ambiguity. True leaders must inspire courage, integrity, trust and personal brilliance in their collegues. Their leadership must be based on their personal character, and must build integrity and character throughout the organisation.

It is to be understood that productivity, performance, profitability and value creation cannot be separated from the dynamics of corporate character. The core group should remember that passion, enthusiasm, creativity, innovativeness, integrity can not be purchased by remuneration-these are required to be cultivated through inspiration and right corporate character as President A P J Abdul Kalam rightly advised: "A virtuous man alone can hear the soul's inner voice clearly. In a wicked man, this faculty is dead. The sensitive nature of his conscience has been destroyed by corruption. Hence, he is unable to discriminate right from wrong. This applies also to organisations, business enterprises, institutions and governments."

Vedanta has also explained the importance of values for human fulfilment. According to Vedanta, the three streams of energy—physical science, the science of values and the science of spirituality-must get synergised for human fulfilment. Vedanta considers the science of values as the link between the physical sciences and science of spirituality.

Convergence of Fundamental Aspects of Character

Corporate character has to be considered as the most important capital. Contribution / effectiveness of all others resources and processes absolutely depends on the organisation character. Unless it is accepted sincerely, no organisation can contribute for socio-economic value creation.

The core group has to align with core values / purpose / priorities and create the context for socio-economic value creation.

Corporate personality has to be built aligning with the core values and basic character of the organisation.

An organization of purpose is an organization of courage, creative expression, conscious awareness and abundant possibility through authentic being and clear compassionate service, and to achieve this **'convergence or creative synthesis/alignment'** of the fundamental aspects of the CORPORATE CHARACTER is required. Only then a socio-economic value creation institution can be built.

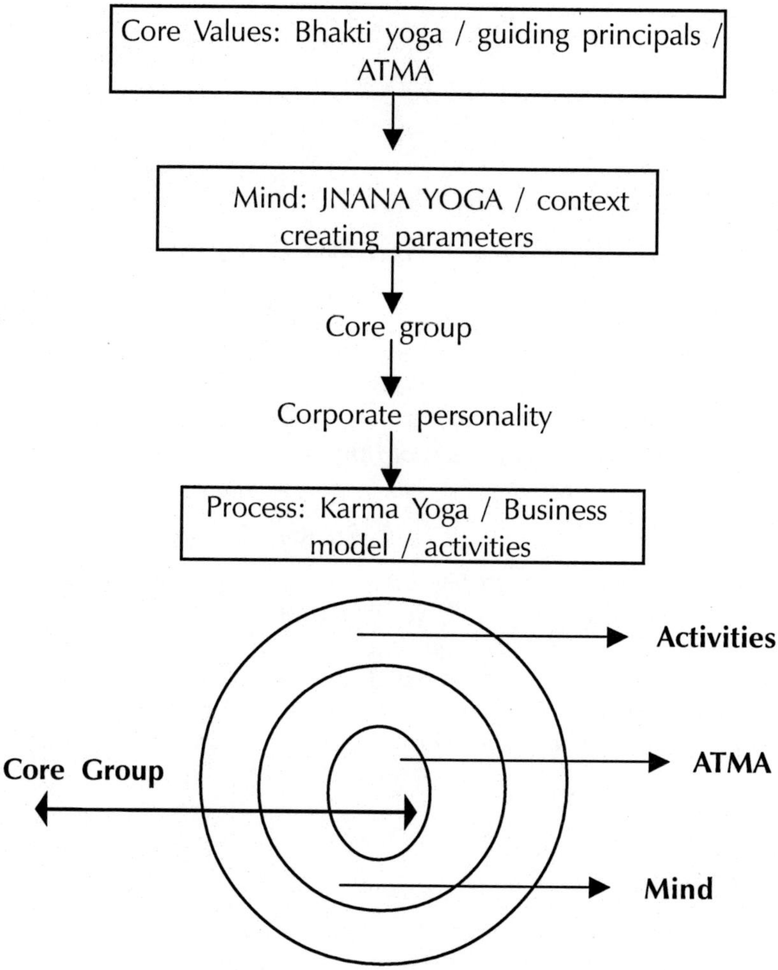

Figure 3.5: Convergence

4

Business Knowledge/Theories & Value Creation

Brother, what shall I do with a mere bread-winning education? I would rather acquire that wisdom that would illuminate my heart and give me satisfaction foreever.

Sri Ramakrishna Paramhansa

Most management philosophy that you read in a book or learn in a class room is going to have limited effectiveness. Once you factor in human beings-egos and personalities-even the most sensible theories begin to fall part..........Management philosphies and management theories are always topped by real life.-**Mark H. McCormack in** *'What Don't Teach you at Harward Business School.'*

Marketing

Recently there was an news item published in a newspaper: " Whirlpool of India in a pool of mess"-a white goods market leader lost money, market share and finally its Managing Director. The company's net profit reduced from 22.45 crore in 2000 to (-) 33.64 in 2003. This is the whole problem. These are confusing times for marketeers. Old tacks like USP and positioning are not working anymore. Expensively maintained brands are proving to be too vulnerable when faced by low cost alternatives—be they from small companies in countries like India, or the in-store brands of US retailers. So called MNC or global FMCG is facing a real crisis due to competition from local brands or low cost options and also from retailers and private labels. They are continuously losing their marketing muscle power to dictate the terms in the market place:

- They have lost their pricing power.
- Low cost options are giving them stiff competition
- Retailers have started exerting in terms of promotion policy, pricing and quality aspects and have also started promoting private labels.

Most of the companies have started realising:

- Urgent requirement of transformation of whole organisation
- Continuous innovation to offer low cost options
- Reduction of costs
- Real respect for customer value
- Respect for retailers and distribution channels' wisdom

If we analyse in depth all these are nothing but the essence of socio-economic value creation model. Without creating socio-economic value no company will be able to withstand the market shock and survive meaningfully. It has already started. Marketing theory or brand theory in its classical form are becoming irrelevant. Traditional marketing methods are not working, even Philip Kotler indirectly acknowledged this in his new book 'Ten Deadly Marketing Sins.'

Kotler has tried to blame marketing practices instead of the theory. We do not understand how even the so-called excellent companies have failed to practice or implement the correct maketing theory? If marketing theory of Kotler is so difficult to practice then what purpose this theory serves? Even established national brands are struggling to get an adequate premium to cover brand-building costs. Even CRM is not working.

As per Kotler, careful application of the segmentation, targeting, and positioning strategy along with 4P's (product, price, place, promotion) strategy helps drive businesses on the track,but he laments, "too many marketing departments do not handle this whole process today. It's handled by a mix of marketers, strategists, financial types, and operations people (As a result) most marketing is reduced to a one-P function-promotion-and not a four –P job. "As per him the whole problem is with the system, process and practices. Hence a new book –*'Ten Deadly Sins.'*

If we carefully study those ten sermons, they are nothing but refinement of old theories in light of the past failures / introspection. We do not understand what is the meaning of careful application, and how it will measure effectiveness. What is the guarantee that these deadly sins will be rectified in practice and what should be the application procedure. Ten Deadly Sins are:

1. Your company is not sufficiently market-focussed and customer driven.
2. Your company does not fully understand its target customers.
3. Your firm needs to better define and monitor its competitors.
4. Your company has not properly managed its relationships with its stakeholders.
5. Your company is not good at finding new opportunities.

6. Your company's marketing planning process is deficient.
7. Your company's product and service policies need tightening.
8. Your company's brand building and communication skills are weak.
9. Your company is not well organized to carry on effective and efficient marketing.
10. Your company has not made maximum use of technology.

All the above issues were considered under marketing discipline. But in reality these issues can't be tackled by the marketing model. It requires involving management, strategic model, core values of the company, resources of the company, context and people. Ultimately, it boils down to corporate character. Corporate character has to be transformed, otherwise nothing will work and Kotler has to define and redefine his theories continuously. Problem is not with practice and procedure or application but the basis or premise of the theories and the context for application. Both depend on the character of the organisation.

In one of the recent interviews Kotler rightly reinterpreted /redefined his famous 4P's theory which is basically nothing but socio-economic value creation:

Old P	New meaning/definition
Product	Customer value
Price	Customer cost
Place	Cusomer convenience
Promotion	Customer communication

Figure: 4.1 Interpretation of P

Some other generally suggested **P's** which are propagated:

- Packaging
- People
- Personnel
- Politics
- Public Opinion
- Passion
- Process
- Physical Evidence
- Product Design
- Penetration
- Positioning

Some people started questioning the very basis of the 4 P's theory and the relevance and I quote from Lior Arussy's interview : "Corporations around the world believe in the four P's of Marketing (product, place, promotion and price). Each and everyone is challenged by new forces. You can match prices and promotions easily. Placements become irrelevant because people can achieve it over the web very quickly anywhere, anytime. Products are even sold as private labels. All these four which are corporate based are gone. They are commodities. What we are promoting to our customers are customer action-based P's-premium price, portion of budget, permanence and preference. These are things that the customer tells you not through perceptions but action....."

One of the important marketing tools–Branding / brand equity is losing its importance / relevance. Branding concept is driven by an organisation's mindset that places market valuation ahead of providing better products / services and achieving customer trust and maintaining customer relationship. Ultimately organization has to create trust by creating value for the customer in a true sense, not just exploiting pseudo-psychology of customer. Communication to authenticate and validate the products / services should be transparent / genuine. Choice, price and convenience outweigh brand in most of the purchasing decision.

Zig Zigler's prescription is quite relevant for brand management : In building a name, you start with being honest. If people think you are honest, they instinctively will trust you and therefore, will be far more likely to listen, and have an interest in you. Trust is the key ingredient in long term successful balanced relationships and business building. Given the current level of consumer cynicism, honesty becomes even more important. A person will buy from a salesperson the first time because they have a need, or the product is superb, or the salesperson is very persuasive. But they will make their second purchase only if the sales person and the product delivers everything that they were represented to do. If they consistently do that, they will have a lifetime customer.

Transparent information sharing is one of the most important parameters for establishing the trust of the customers and society at large towards the organisation and its product / services. Greed should not guide the information strategy of the organisation. This should be based on ethics and social good. The information strategy defines the way an organisation shares its strengths and weaknesses, both in business and its products and services. It is never asked for by the customers since most of the customers are not aware of the complex processes or technologies and the inside functioning of the companies.

By sharing the information transparently an organisation can make real difference in terms of reputation and image of the organisation. Organisation should realise 'perception is reality' and the positive perception can be established only by sharing information transparently.

Information sharing strategy ultimately depends on the commitment of the 'core group' of the organisation. It is a startegic business decision since it involves the future of the company and requires investments to sustain.

To build long term trust of the customers and the society, an organisation should avoid 'confused communication syndrome'.

Professor Jagdish Sheth had suggested the importance of three A's of Marketing. As per him,every consumer has three customers within him-buyer, payer and user. As a user, the customer seeks psychological and functional attributes from the product; as a payer the customer seeks accessibility, which means the product or brand has to be accessible when the customer looks for it. The customer experience becomes crucial at the level of accessibility, for that is when the customer is accessing the product. That is the time when marketers have to build the experiential element. Three A's of marketing as suggested by Professor Sheth : Adaptability, Accessibility and affordability. As per him a brand should be able to align within the 3A marketing framework to be successful.

Several organisations are losing market share and their bottomlines are under pressure inspite of several branding strategies / tactics are being continuously adopted. Market dynamics have changed drastically due to socio-economic forces as well as access of information, flow of information in a much more democratic manner and the vast change in the mindset of the consumers, and thus without value creation no amount of the so-called brand strategy will work.

Organisation must have heart. People & society have to be the centre of all activities. This is nothing but socio-economic value creation.

There are serious debates among the marketing gurus also. At the one end, there are academics like Danniel Kahneman and Harvard's Gerald Zaltman who insist that most marketing theories professional jargons with little or no mooring in science and thus doomed anyway. How can one, he says try to sell to today's consumers without understanding how the brain processes messages. And then, at the other end, there are gurus like Kotler and Ries who insist that traditional marketing theory works. It is just that companies are not implementing it properly. Main problem is implementation. It is a paradox that with so many highly intelligent CEOs / marketing executives and consultants—how 'implementation'is still the main problem or an issue?

Kelly Mooney had prescribed 10 parameters in her book, *'The Ten Demandments'* to make marketing effective and deliver as per expectations of the companies. These Ten Demandments are:

1. Earn my trust
2. Inspire me
3. Make it easy
4. Put me in charge
5. Guide me
6. 24/7...
7. Get to know me
8. Exceed my expectations
9. Reward me
10. Stay with me

Mooney had cited several examples of firms and sectors to explain her parameters. She observed that executives in most of the companies speak about being customer-centric but in reality most still fail to deliver. In interviewing several executives for her book, she found three common parameters for success:

- Leadership with a sense of urgency
- Role-modelling customer-centric behaviour
- Accountability and rewards

However, she observed that most of the company culture and processes are required to be shifted from the boardroom to the mail room and that has not happened. A stumbling block in taking the Demandments through the company is sometimes due to the middle management-either because the company is not communicating its message or the team lacks the experience and mind-set to initiate change. But, as per Mooney, the maximum resistance is invariably at the highest level. It takes a lot of time and a very committed CEO. Its not always the case since companies are run by executives doing things the same way.

Mooney recommended that marketing be regarded not as a separate silo but something that integrates with customer service, operations and data base management.

If we analyse Kotler's 10 Deadly sins and Mooney's Ten Demandments or Jagdish Sheth's 3A's, there is no fundamental difference. The real issue is implementation. All the mouthful parameters in reality cannot be implemented unless the balancesheet-mindset is transformed into a socio-economic value creation mind-set and for this transformationto occur, corporate character has to be reoriented or transformed. That is the crux. Nothing else will work.

Management

Transformation of corporate character basically means liberation of character so that context creating resources can be utilised to their full potential. Without the utilization of resources no organization can become a value generation institution. Even Peter Drucker, the greatest management thinker of our time, has accepted the importance of liberation of Planned abandonment

- Focus on opportunities
- Preserving values
- Learning from non-profit organisation

Peter Drucker also advised: "The proof of the sincerity and seriousness of a management is uncompromising emphasis on integrity of character. This, above all, has to be symbolised in the management's "people" decisions. For, it is character through which leadership is exercised; it is character that sets the example and is imitated. Align yourself with people who have integrity.

The most important work of the executive is to identify the changes that have already happened. The important challenge in society, economics, politics, is to exploit the changes that have already occurred. The important thing is to identify the "future that has already happened"-and to develop a methodology for perceiving and analysing these changes.

All organisations need to know that virtually no activity will perform effectively for a long time without modification and redesign....Effective executives know that they have to get many things done effectively. Therefore, they concentrate, and the first rule for the concentration of executive efforts is to slough off the past that has ceased to be productive. The first-class resources, especially those scarce resources of human strength, are immediately pulled out and put to work on the opportunities of tomorrow. If leaders are unable to slough off yesterday, to abandon yesterday, they simply will not be able to create tomorrow...Stop squandering resources on obsolete businesses and free up your capable people to take advantage of new opportunities."

Management gurus like C. K. Prahalad and Stuart Hart have been pointing towards the "bottom of the pyramid", the four billion people, who have very low incomes. The poor comprise the world's largest untapped market. As per Prahalad poor people who are living under $2 a day represent a new market. This market needs to be accessed and approached somewhat differently than the traditional market. Once we consider them as consumers, we have the obligation to treat them with respect. As per him, the future profitability of MNCs and Indian private sector ventures entirely depend on this market. This is not an option, but a necessity. But this is not possible without transforming the character of the organisation and accepting the socio-economic value creation approach.

What is the use of writers,gurus,books, theories and jargons unless these generate socio-economic value? Why will the society bother? Why the society will respect unless it serves a social purpose except this, which creates market for the intellectual to survive and make money.

What Mulk Raj Anand beautifully described in *'On the Real Test of the Novelist'* is aptly applicable for all intellectuals: "It may lie in the transformation of words into prophecy. Because, what is a writer if he is not the fiery voice of the people, who through his own torments,urges and exaltations, by realizing the pains, frustrations and aspirations of others, and by cultivating his incipient powers of expression, transmutes in art all feeling, all thought, all experience—thus becoming the seer of a new vision in any given situation."

Roi / Roc Debate

Another concept as an extension of CRM has been introduced and marketed by Pepper and Rogers Group, a mangement consulting firm. They are suggesting to replace ROI strategy by ROC (Return On Customer). ROC is defined as the rate at which a business creates value from any given amount of customer lifetime values. Customer can create value for firm in two ways : they can return current-period profits, or they can become more loyal or valuable, ensuring that future-period profits will increase. This second way results in an increase in the customer's lifetime value.

As prescribed by the Pepper and Rogers Group, ROC involves changing everything about how the present-day businesses organise themselves and how they measure and reward performance. As per the present model, companies measure their success interms of current profit. They do not measure their ROC and can't be held accountable for it. This sometimes results in companies destroying a great deal of their own value in their mindless quest for current income.

Companies need to change their perspective from Return On Investment (ROI) to Return on Customer (ROC), thus giving more weightage to the customer and deriving maximum value from it. As Pepper said : "You have to see things more and more from the customers's perspective, put yourself into customer's shoes, and you must literally become the customer yourself. Only by treating the customer the way you would want to be treated if you were the customer can you actually maximise your ROC".

A firm needs to cultivate a culture of customer trust, so as to maximise its ROC in long term value at the fastest possible rate. It is only when the customer trusts the firm to act in his own interest that the firm would maximize the return on customer.

This concept also indirectly accepts the socio-economic value creation, but still is focussed on targeting customer's satisfaction maximisation. How to create that long term value? We cannot ignore the short term. You have to survive in the short term also. You have to see the things from the socio-economic perspective. You have to offer products / services with socio-economic solutions. Mere customer focus will not help. Customers are not really aware of the unlimited potential of value creation. ROI is also important. You have to make your investment efficient and effective. Your technology choice has to be creative. Your production process should be efficient.

Customer loyalty in both short term and long term is equally important. Customer loyalty and social trust cannot be achieved without genuine value creation and this cannot be done without corporate character. Ignoring this, no concept will work. This will become another fad which everybody will forget after sometime or, it will be replaced by a new concept or fad.

Organisation Structure and value creation

It is important to build a team, rather than worry about the perfect structure. Organization structures in real life never resemble neat boxes that are used to depict them on paper. The key driving force, lies ironically outside the structure-how are people going to creatively collabotare across different departments which will generate value. How the core team will connect with each other and work as a cohesive team. How are they going to motivate and sustain such behaviour etc.

Creativity and innovation should not be leader- or organization structure-centric. It finally depends on the corporate character of the company. "Organisation charts and fancy titles count for next to nothing" was observed by Colin Powell in the *'Leadership Primer'*. He also explained "organization charts are frozen,anachronistic photos in a work place that ought to be as dynamic as the external environment around you. If people really followed organization charts, companies would collapse. In well- run organisations, titles are pretty meaningless. At best,they advertise some authority, an official status conferring the ability to give orders and induce obedience. But titles mean little in terms of real power, which is the capacity to influence and inspire....."

Most ideas are generated when people exchange information. It is essential to create a social engine,a structure that allows information to flow in the right channels throughout the organization. Innovation itself is a social process where everyone can participate. Value creation should be averybody's business.

Mark H. Mc Cormack observed: "Companies never function according to their organisational charts. They are made up people and personalities and politics and powerplays, none of which can be connected by solid or dotted lines".

Convergence of socio-economic value creation / ethics and sustained business model-is there any contradiction?

There is absolutely no contradiction but a confusion created by the so-called experts and business leaders who want to avoid any sort of social accountability. On the contrary these three are complementary to each other. No amount of 'intelligence' of CEOs / leaders can ensure the sustained business model without the convergence of these three. In the 21st century no company can finally survive without this convergence since information, knowledge or ideas are nobody's monopoly. The civic community's pressure is increasing day-by-day and the customer is becoming more knowledgeable. Moreover, for growth new customers have to be created and brought in the 'market.'

In reality, it is possible and already some companies have taken the initiative and made an excellent contribution and some others are in the process. Aravinda Eye Hospital, AMUL, HDFC, ITCs E-Choupal, Chaupal Sagar initiative, initiative by Raj Reddy-to name a few who have successfully done the convergence. Ethics is an integral part of value creation. Similarly 'surplus cannot be created either economically or socially without an efficient business model. These are complimentary and not contradictory as people are trying to propagate. HDFC demonstrated that a wholesome business, meeting an important social need,can also be extremely profitable.

Socio-economic value creation depends on 'core purpose' and the mind of the organisation.There is no contradiction between value creation and business.Product/services should be with socio-economic insights or solutions.

Aravinda Eye Hospital near Madurai is one of the excellent examples of a socio-economic value creation institution. This is the story which proves that through transformation of corporate character, a great institution can be built. Absolute commitment and genuine compassion can create socio-economic value not the CSR or lip service. With continuous improvement and innovation they have reduced the cost of a routine cataract operation 2000-5000. They are continuosly increasing the number of centers as well as employing the local people, training them, and involving them. They are giving leadership and motivating the civic society. They are constantly developing people with vision and the ability io implement vision.

Amul movement is one of the excellent examples of sustainable rural development. Anand, a small town in Gujarat has emerged as India's milk capital. It was here that an experiment in co-operative dairying launched nearly six decades back, revolutionised Indian dairying and helped India become the largest milk producer in the world. The Amul model has been hailed as the role model for transforming the rural economy in India and for setting up a sustainable institution, which has a holistic approach to improve the quality of life with a tangible and measureable impact. Following main factors contributed to the success of Amul movement:

- The farmers owned the dairy.
- Their elected representatives managed the village societies and the district unions.
- They employed professionals to operate the dairy and manage its business.
- The co-operatives were sensitive to the needs of the farmers and responsive to their demands.

In 1965 the National Dairy Development Board was set up with the basic objective of replicating the Amul Model of cooperative dairying, thus ensuring that the farmer members control procurement, processing and marketing. The Amul model of dairy development is a three tiered structure with the dairy cooperative societies at the village level federated under a milk union at the district level and a federation of member unions at the state level.

Over the last four decades, more than 11 million farmers have joined one lakh village dairy cooperative societies linked to nearly 180 processing unions spread throughout India inspired by the Amul Model. These cooperatives own some of the largest business enterprises in the country. For example, 2.3 million farmers of Gujarat own India's largest food products marketing organisation, the Gujarat Cooperative Milk Marketing Federation with an annual sales turnover of about Rs.3000 crores. Some of the largest brands in dairying are owned by the cooperatives. The Amul model has helped create strong cooperative brands like Vijaya, Verka, Sudha, Saras, Milma and many more.

Amul model is a great example of socio-economic value creation for sustained rural development. It uses the potential of rural population, promotes the community feeling, liberates the rural population from the clutches of vested interests, ensures dignity of life and sustained increase in living standard.

ITC's 'e-choupal' is a business driven initiative that makes a difference to society at a national level,by helping reduce poverty and creating sustainable livelihood opportunities. ITC's 'e-choupal' initiative is an attempt to create socio-economic value. ITC has created crop-specific content-rich local language websites with its enormous knowledge base in agriculture. To enable farmers to readily access these local websites right in their villages, ITC has set up internet kiosks, or e-choupal installations, in rural hinterland. Farmers can instantly ascertain the prevalent Indian and international prices and price trends for their crops,learn the best practices in cultivation, get expert knowledge and advice, buy agricultural inputs like fertilizers and pesticides online, and also get to know the micro level weather forecast.

It empowers farmers with an expert knowledge by innovatively leveraging information technology. It provides farmers real time access to customised knowledge on specially designed websites in their own languages-helping them align farm output to market demands and secure better quality, productivity and improved price realisation. The 'e-choupal' is already empowering over 3 million farmers through 4,100 installations covering 30000 villages across six states of India. Over the next decades, ITC plans to cover 100,000 villages, representing one-sixth of India's villages to create more than 10 million e-farmers. E-choupals have the potential to convert village populations into vibrant economic organizations. The e-choupal network builds a unique low-cost fulfilment capacity for two-way flow of goods and services in and out of Indian villages. In turn, this creates a unique opportunity, for creating new markets and generating economic surplus.

ITC has also embraced the rural retail model and plans to put up stores called Choupal Sagars, each catering to 100 villages. The first Choupal Sagar in Sehore (MP) is already operational. ITC plans to have 1000 of such Choupal Sagars, with 50 of them scheduled to be set up in the first year itself at an investment of Rs150 crores. Choupal Sagar offers multiple services under one roof at a tractorable distance from the villager's house. It houses a soil testing laboratory, farmer training centre, medical consultation and diagnostic facilities, a restaurant, a store selling quality products for both farm and household consumption and banking and insurance services.

Raj Reddy, a pioneering researcher in artificial intelligence and a professor at Carnegie Mellon University, plans to unveil within one year his new project, called the PCtvt, a $ 250 wirelessly networked personal computer intended for four billion people around the world who live on less than $2000 a year. This device can find a market in developing countries particularly those with large populations of people who cannot read, because it can be controlled by a simple TV remote control and can function as a television, telephone and videophone. Because his low-cost Computer doubles as a TV and a DVD player, Reddy believes that he will be able to use it as a vehicle to take computing and communications to populations that until now have been excluded from the digital world. This is the socio-economic value creation approach which believes that even poorest people can become a profitable market for computer

Business is for making money. Business is not for philanthrophy or social development. Business development depends on how manipulative you are. Business is ethics or values neutral. These are all self-defeating assumptions or perceptions which will be extremely harmful for the organisation in the 21st century given the tremendous pressure of social, economical and political and market forces a company has to withstand. A corporation has to increase the social acceptance index and reduce the social distrust index drastically.

If corporations serve customers well, provide products or services of extraordinary quality, and unlock the full potential of their employees to fulfill themselves and the organisation's core values or purpose, shareholders' interest is automatically protected. This paradigm shift will be the driving force for future survival and growth.

Generally corporate, social and environmental initiatives tend to be philanthropic and hence limited in scale and genuine effort. However, above creative initiatives have demonstrated that there is no inherent contradiction between the objectives of creating shareholder value and enhancing social and environmental resources. The above initiatives are trying to ensure that these two objectives mutually dovetail into and reinforce each other. The more the synergy, the more sustainable will be the model of growth and development.

We should remember that there are beliefs or perceptions which have more to do with people's predilections and prejudices than with the ground realities. There is no dichotomy between profit and ethics. Only we are required to transform our mindset and understanding. As Plato observed : "we can easily forgive a child who is afraid of the dark. The real tragedy of life is when men are afraid of the light."

Information explosion and customer power

Through much of the past century, advertisement has mainly catered to a captive audience confined to just a few radios or television channels or a limited number of publications. Now media choice has exploded too, and consumers select what they want from a far greater variety of sources—especially with a few clicks of a computer mouse.Thanks to the internet, the consumer is finally seizing power.

Consumer power has profound implications for companies. Many firms already claim to be "consumer-driven" or "consumer-centric". Now their claims will be tested as never before. Trading on consumers' ignorance will no longer be possible : people will know and soon tell others, even those without the internet-that prices in the next town are cheaper or that certain goods are inferior. The internet is working wonders in raising standards. Good and honest firms should benefit most. But it is also intensifying competition. Today, window shopping takes place online. People can compare products, prices and reputations. Newspapers / magazines and websites constantly review products and services.

This is changing the nature of consumer decisions. Until recently, consumers usually learned about a product and made their choice at the same time. People would often visit a department store or dealership to seek advice from a salesman, look at his recommendation and then buy. Now for many each of these steps is separate. As per some survey, 80% of customers have already used the internet to decide what car they want to buy and what they are willing to pay even before they arrive at a showroom.

Of course, the amount of time people spend researching and checking prices tends to rise in proportion to the value of the product. Consumers are displaying similar behaviour when they purchase other things,such as digital cameras, mobile phones, fashionable items or packaged goods from a supermarket. Customers are better informed than ever before about the value or health implications of the products sold in the supermarket. Reaching these better-informed consumers with a marketing message is not easy, and not only because they are more sceptical. Many people now spend as much time surfing the web as they do with television, magazines or newspapers. The audience for advertising is splintering and its attention is harder to attract.

Many companies do not yet seem aware of the implications of newly empowered consumers. It is true that the vast majority of people still go to shops for most purchases. Before doing that, however, most have used the internet. Internet has already provided explosion of choice to the consumers. But the consumer's choice is about to become even greater. Internet search firms such as Google, Yahoo! and MSN are now falling over each other to offer more localised services. These promise to open up new goldmines in search advertising. And soon this facility will be available not just on PCs at home or work, but on mobile phones. At a touch, consumers will be able to find a local store and then check the offers from nearby outlets even as they browse the aisles, or listen to a sales man. When that happens consumers will truly be kings, and only those firms ready and able to serve these 'new powerful consumers' will survive.

Two-way linked integration model

For building a socio-economic value generation institution, a two-way linked model is required to be developed and nurtured. Corporate character, corporate strategy (business model) and corporate activities (processes) are to be creatively converged. The core group has to ensure continuous interaction with each other in a dynamic situation to achieve proper synthesis and convergence.

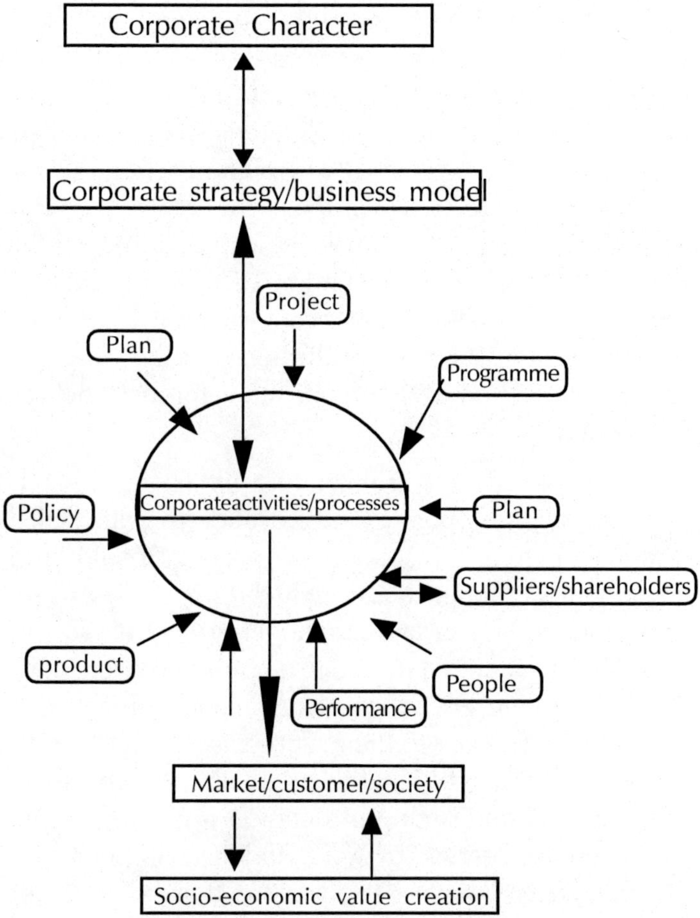

Figure 4.2: The Two-way linked model

Value creation : Speed and integration

Any organisation, for sustained value creation, must have speed and flexibility to ensure the cooperation and integration of all aspects of the business on real-time basis to anticipate and respond to the changes in the environment. Speed and integration is the driver for sustained value creation.

Survival and growth in the uncertain and complex business environment can be compared to surviving and withstanding the cruel and unforgiving nature of life in the mountain, jungle or desert. It is quite relevant to follow the co-operative and collaborative nature of different species in nature. It is also quite relevant to study how various creatures react with speed in response to signals that could range from shrill signal of a bird or crying of animals indicative of the presence of a predator, to that of an impending earthquake, cyclone or any natural calamity. During the recent tsunami, it has been proved that the animals / birds got the sense of the disaster much in advance and tried to communicate it through their abnormal behaviour.

There is a lesson from nature which is relevant for the organisation: co-operate and collaborate with stakeholders, and anticipate and respond to signals that could be threat or opportunity. Organisations which are achieving excellent performance in a sustained manner are extremely efficient in collecting,analysing and understanding the data / information of the dynamic environment and taking proactive response with speed. The key to their success is the ability to anticipate and understand the signal in the reality and the speed of the proactive action. Timing of decision and action is extremely important as observed by Anita Roddick, Founder, Body Shop: "I am aware that success is more than a good idea. It is timing too."

Market is neutral. It does not show any mercy to anybody. The most important issue is how to share knowledge / information / data accross the value chain on a real-time basis. To achieve this following key aspects are required to be made integral parts of the organisation:

- Speed
- Integration

- Collaboration
- Synchronisation
- Interpretation & utilisation

Speed and the integration are the keys to outsmart the competition in the dynamic business environment.

'Knowledge' of how to use and integrate the information / data or knowledge on real-time basis is fundamental. Along with knowledge, the organisation has to restructure its physical collaborative relationship infrastructure to integrate suppliers, customers and other stakeholders where everybody can interact and respond on a real-time basis. Organisation is required to build a proactive real-time mutually beneficial relationship network which links business processes of independent organisational units in a uniform manner. This network can draw on the strength of each individual stakeholder to generate shared benefits for all the stakeholders. All the partners interact with each other in the network in real-time which ensures proactive response to a changed situation with speed and in a trustworthy manner. Organisation that can get the synergy of all the efforts of collaborative stakeholders will be able to withstand the unceratainty of business and to ensure a sustained value creation. Stan Davis observed : "As the information economy comes of age, a surprising thing is happening : information systems are starting to take their cues from biological ones. Information is converging with biology, and business is following suit. Biology is not the only system that evolves; and the concepts of evolution help to explain the process of change in any connected system, be it the ecology or the economy. Our institutions, business included, have been built for stability, not for change. As connectivity proceeds, business leaders face an imperative to create organizations that can adapt continually and rapidly, to keep space with shifts in their markets, technologies, and society itself. It is the world of biology that holds the key to meeting that imperative......... The hyper-connected information economy has led to new assaults on privacy. What has been less well observed is that connectivity has created the marked increase in economic volatility that will define the key challenges of the next decade."

Any organisation wanting to be information / knowledge /data driven, has to make the following integral parts of the business strategy:

- Simplify
- Standardise
- Automate

One of the best ways to simplify business operations is to consolidate information / knowledge /data. Businesses need to know how their supply chain is faring, how quickly inventory is moving, what competitors are doing, what is the technology trend and what is the market trend etc. To get the complete picture of its customers and its business, companies have to simplify. All business systems must be connected, and all business applications must share a single repository of customers, products, service information, and more. This will make information available on a real-time basis.

A key enabling force that an organisation should adopt to standardise operation is to implement highly efficient business applications, which include proven business pratices, using open, readily available applications which reduces costs, streamlines management maintenance, and increases business effectiveness and efficiency.

What distinguishes Information Age business from prior models is a much higher level of automation. The new businesses are driven by world-class applications. Older model businesses provided only partial process automation. They were task-specific and designed to tackle little jobs here and there. This created fragmented data everywhere, preventing further automation at the enterprise level. System should collect, process, and share information from all lines of business. Business processes should be automated so that information/data is shared instantly and puts and makes, available all the business information one place.

Information has become the most powerful capital today. However, information will be useful for the society if it is transformed into knowledge / wisdom. Vidyut Joshi rightly suggested in an article *'Emergence of Information Society'*: "However, mere use of information does not ensure a problem-free society. Data becomes meaningful only when it is information. When information, is useful, it becomes knowledge and when knowledge is used to create a better society, it becomes wisdom."

5

Role of Corporate/Management Community

In today's corporate world leaders say something and they do something completely different, thereby losing credibility.-
Infosys Chairman quoted in the Economic Times.

N. R. Narayana Murthy

Great management and great people are the most important elements for success. Sustained success, however, requires integrity, courage, trust, openness and true meritocracy at all levels.-

James Dimon, CEO, Bank One

Value creation and corporate community

The corporate sector has to change its business approach if it really wants to survive, grow and contribute to the social good. There has to be a collective role. For its survival the market has to expand organically i.e new customers should be brought in the market net. This is possible by giving job opportunities to the people so that purchasing power can be generated. Opportunities can be given by redistributing knowledge information among the masses. Rushi C. Bakshi wrote in an article : "the corporates, therefore, need to be sensitive to socio-political issues, role of social enterprises in the global ordernot only as a corporate social responsibility but also for long term profitability and survival. This realisation is only now downing on much of the corporate world. Therefore, there is a yet unrecognised but significant corporate demand for manageri al resources, which understands the social dynamics."

Only internet / IT / computers will not create much jobs. We should not be under illusions. The real future of jobs lies in–Education, health, food, water, sanitation, environment, housing and agriculture, rural development. As per one estimate IT will create about 0.5 million jobs where as India needs about 10 million jobs per year given the present rate of growth of youth population. We are creating more software parks than jobs. We are solving problems of the West. So far we are using Indian talent to solve the problems of the West. It is not even the Western poor, but the Western rich. The best talent in India does not get to solve the problems of the poor. We are much more concerned about the western market than the Indian market.

In India about 1000 large medium size companies are there. There is a huge wastage of resources by the promoters/ CEOs/Board members by their extravagant life style / expenses including their family members as well. Even if they reduce these expenses by 5% several crores people can be brought into the market system within the next 10 years.

All companies are basically financed by general public directly or indirectly or both. Any company operating in any country enjoys the various infrastructure and utility facilities provided by the State-like road, rail, port, communication, law order, property protection, trained educated manpower. All the economic and social infrastructures are developed and maintained by tax payer's money. Hence, the argument that corporation does not have any social responsibility is just cheating the society country. Corporations do not exist in air nor this is an abstract entity. It is very much the part of society and the economic system of the country.

Lavish lifestyles of corporate leaders, CEOs or promoters are advertised in the newspapers on regular basis during the various social events / functions like marriage. Recently, a corporate house is constructing its house which will cost not less than Rs 130 crores, if a newspaper report is to believed. In the recent past some corporate houses spent 50/60 crores *for* their son/daughter's wedding. And in an all-time record or benchmark in extravagant lifestyle recently one corporate tycoon spent xxx 370 crore on his daughter's wedding. It appears that they are not at all concerned about the society or citizen. This is the greatest example of hypocrisy. On one side extreme proverty-even drinking water is not available while on the other side people are using golden glasses to drink mineral water. Corporate community should start thinking about the negative impact of '**competitive extravagant lifestyle**'pursued by most of its members.

Corporate houses generally give such standard excuses:

- Government is inefficient
- Economic reform is very slow
- Government is not extending co-operation etc
- Business is not for social development etc.

But they never take the responsibility or blame themselves. In India about 1000 large and medium size organisations/ corporations are operating. Even if they contribute 5% of their annual profit and constitute a "Socio-economic transformation fund" and manage the fund properly to utilise for:

- Education
- Public Health
- Agriculture
- Rural development
- Drinking water
- Rural sanitaion

Several crores of people will be freed from the vicious circle of proverty within a spare of 10 years. In the ultimate analysis the corporate sector will be benefitted enormously since these people will be able to enter the "market system" and would be purchasing various goods and services. Also a more efficient manpower will be readily available for corporate sector.

Social responsibilty / corporate social responsibility index has become a fad or jargon without much significance since most of the cases, it is for:

- Public relation exercise
- Photo opportunity
- Engaging the wives/daughters
- Philanthropic approach

Time has come when organisations have to accept that corporate entity is partner in the social transfornation exercize and they have to give respect to citizens instead of taking up to dole out mercy. This has to be done for their own survival. As Swami Vivekananda said : "Work for the world only for your salvation". Corporate community is still not much concerned about the civic society / community. But for their own survival and growth, it is high time that they start to introspect on:

- Duality of lifestyle eventually leads to social tension, confusion chaos and law and order problem in the society.
- For growth and profit more number of people should be brought in the market system, otherwise how will the growth be achieved and sustained.
- Co-operation between the civic society and the corporations only can bring social development and equilibrium.
- Corporation should strive for social acceptance / reducing social distrust index.

Baba Amte in an interview explained the role of the corporate sector: "Whoever is powerful in society has a moral obligation towards those not so privileged. Only if they perform their social responsibility can the *taana-baana* (social fabric) be sustained. Corporate India also has a responsibility towards protecting the environment. We have received this earth as a very special endowment for us to preserve and bequeath to generations to come. Will we nurture it for our children or will we pollute our rivers, deplete our ground water and destroy our forests? Corporate India has to face this question with honesty and commitment."

Corporate community should accept the fact that without socio-economic value creation, no harmonious existence is possible for the corporate sector. Social trust cannot be achieved unless integrity is practised in a real sense. It is better to wake up fast, as observed by Kenneth E. Goodpaster, Professor of Business Ethics, at the University of St Thomas, Minneapolis: "Business leaders are the principal architects of corporate conscience. They are the ones who must manage the challenges associated with pursuing profit while maintaining integrity. They are the ones most responsible for delivering on the moral agenda of the corporation. The agenda includes three broad imperatives—orienting, institutionalising, and sustaining ethical values within the corporate culture."

Dr. R.A. Mashelkar has mentioned 'human centred development' as the balance of five e's namely, ecology, environment, economics, equity, and ethics. He has also stated that the word 'equity' must be substituted with 'dignity' and this can come only through the process of self—employment which alone can bring self empowerment.

The corporate community should start involving itself for social development instead of showing charity. The corporate community should be involved actively for overall development besides the growth and development of their respective corporation:

- Rural development
- Education
- Health care
- Drinking water
- Infrastructure
- Sanitation
- Agricultural development

All the business associations should start thinking seriously and have a genuine dialogue among themselves to formulate various programmes and their implementation. A 'social transformation fund' should be formed by contribution from the companies. Certain percentage of turnover / profit to be contributed. Help of leading Business schools is required to be taken to formulate various programmes and strategies to implement, monitor and supervise various programmes.

Civic community also has to be motivated, involved to start a social transformation programme in the true sense.

Corporate community should sincerely accept the advice of Dr. R. A. Mashelkar : "Knowledge without innovation is of no value. It is through the process of innovation that knowledge is converted into wealth and social good. Innovative nations lead the world today. .....Building a globally competitive Indian industry will automatically follow when we get the fundamentals of knowledge and innovation-centric approaches right."

Also for socio-economic value creation, corporate community should sincerely understand the significance and importance of the comments made by Kaushik Basu in a one of his article":....economists typically worry about the big things, like money supply, the balance of trade and budget deficits. These are important, of course,but many economies fail not because of these, but because of the malfunctioning of 'small things'-the nuts and bolts of the economy. We need to work assiduously on injecting efficiency and cutting down corruption in everyday governance. If this is done,it will make life easier for ordinary people, who will then invest in business and enterprise."

Importance of knowledge infrastructure

Corporate community should understand the importance of knowledge / learning infrastructure and try to focus and contribute in this direction.

According to data from the United Nations Population Division, 51 percent of India's population in 2000 was in the age group 20-64, which could be thought of as the potential work force. Of this, some 377 million, or 37 percent of the population, was in the age group 20-44, which one could classify as the younger workforce. By 2030, this 20-44 year group will grow to almost 54 million, or over 38 percent of the country's population. This will be the largest potential work force in the world.

In the knowledge economy, this potential work force needs to be educationally empowered to have a fair chance of being actually employed. To achieve this, huge infrastructure for learning / knowledge is required which is unfortunately missing. As per some study, the ground reality:

- Only 53 percent of rural habitations in India have primary schools i.e 1-5 standard.
- Only 18 percent of primary schools in rural India have four or more teachers.
- Only 18 percent of rural India has upper primary schools i.e 6-8 standard.
- There are less than 64000 secondary schools and 23000 secondary schools in rural India

Reality is that we do not have in place even a basic school education infrastructure for the vast rural population. How will the majority of the population be come engaged in meaningful economic activities? How will the corporate sector get effective and efficient manpower during the next 15/20 years? Corporate sector has to play a major role to prepare the future knowledge workers for their own interest and the society. A major initiative is required to be taken in this direction without losing further time.

For sustainable development, education is the most important factor as the United Nations rightly advised : for the next decade we should focus on education for sustainable development. Development that meets the needs of the present without compromising the ability of future generations to meet their own needs and which focusses towards socio-economic value creation is sustainable development.

For sustainable development which creates socio-economic value, a transformation within human beings themselves is required. Only transformation and reorientation of human beings will enable us to meet the challenges that face us. To achieve this education needs to focus on developing:

- Sense of integrity
- Compassion
- Sense of responsibility
- Courage, and
- Wisdom.

Swami Vivekananda said : "Education is not the amount of information that is put into your brain and runs riot there, undigested all your life. You must have life-building, man-making, character-making, assimilation of ideas. If you have assimilated five ideas and made them your life and character, you have more education than any man who has got by heart a whole library. If education were identical with information, the libraries would be the greatest sages in the world and encyclopaedias the Rishis."

Success of education for sustainable development will depend on whether it can touch people's lives at all strata of society. If the bottom of the society is outside the socio-economic development, it will not serve the real purpose and in the long run this will result in social disharmony and chaos.

As per census figures, about 17.2% of India's graduates are jobless. The number of jobless in India increased by more than three times in 10 years—from 13.8 million in 1991 to 44.5 million in 2001. The unemployment rate of graduates is significantly higher than the overall unemploment rate of 10.1%. The census also showed that over 4200 graduates had been reduced to begging or vagrancy.

This data clearly indicates our educational system is in a total mess. The information / knowledge economy has no use of bookish knowledge or marks oriented education system. Correlation between college / university education system and the proper development of skills and works required in the economy has to be established to clear this mess. Creation of a relevant skilled labour force is the most critical issue. Corporate sector should take the initiative to influence the government as well as the society at large in this direction. This has to be done for their own interest otherwise from where they will get the efficient manpower to propel the developmental affort..

Education must create responsible future citizens. Education must have a human face. Observations of E. Balagurusamy, Vice-Chancellor, Anna University are quite relevant in this regard: "...I strongly believe that we have to solve the problems of society. Universities should become proactive; the attitude of doing something for society is very important. We have the ability but we don't project a positive attitude.......You have to be a good human being; otherwise all the knowledge you gained has no meaning. You need ethics and values or else, you will not able to serve the society. This should be an integral part of the learning process...Basic reasearch is important but it should be translated into helping society and social needs."

Character of B-School and value creation

In our B-Schools 'society' is missing. All sorts of courses are being taught there—business strategy, marketing management, market segmentation study, customer behaviour study, pricing model, brand management, demand estimation, financial management, HR management etc etc. However, hardly any course is there which deals with social-economic value creation or concern for the society or citizen. They have started becoming isolated from the social reality and eventually started thinking they are living on some other planet. They are not at all familiar with the socio-economic value creation equation. The whole culture of B school—this is not even been discussed. They are taught to be intellectually professionally cunning not socially responsive or concerned. The concern for society or country is terribly missing in the whole game of business /management education. In reality the mission/vision objectives of the students in general are:

- To maximise self –interest.
- Too much concern for career.
- To go up the corporate ladder at any cost.
- Too much concern for salary/perks

From this kind of educational factories, you will get only profit-oriented managers or so-called leaders and their contribution to socio-economic value creation would be incidental. Already debate has started regarding relevance of management education and the contribution of B-schools in value addition. The main criticisms are:

- Failure in soft skills -Emotional Quotient development
- Concentration in analytical ability
- Emotional/personal attributes are ignored
- Students have short term objective-getting best job at any cost
- No importance is given to their overall development as human being.

Some of the B-schools are trying to develop emotional and personality attributes through 'Spiritual Quotient' which is a sum of EQ and IQ. But in reality this is just a drop in the ocean. Two main issues are being debated among the management intellectuals

- Management education should focus on moral values / ethics
- Management education should focus only on profit & loss aspects of the business

There seems to be no consensus among them yet on this. There is total confusion and everybody is having their own articulated intellectual justification. As per one group of management intellectuals, B-schools have attempted to elevate business management to a science which has led to simplistic models of human behaviour based on self-maximising utility. A fall out of this is the creation of a moral vacuum in corporate houses, which has led to a proliferation of Enron-type scandals. As per them much of management theory places too much reliance on maximising profits to the detriment of ethics and morality. The only thing that motivates MBAs is the profit curve which is required to be changed on an urgent basis. The focus should be shifted to ethics and moral values and this should become integral parts of the management education.

Another group of intellectuals believes that blaming errant behaviour in the business world on the MBA system is a convenient way of detracting from the core issue-the breakdown of human values. To put the blame squarely on the kind of business education is not justified. Ethical principles are not a list of dos and don'ts to be learnt in classrooms and applied to the real world for they become worthless when taken out of context. A professional course is meant to instruct on the mechanics of business predicted on profit and loss. The human angle and ethics are subjective and hence cannot be taught in classrooms.

This type of intellectual debate only increases the confusion and diverts attention from the real issue. It is not justified to make business education or MBA system solely responsible for the irresponsible behaviour in the corporate sector. Business schools or MBAs are also a part of the whole corporate sector. MBAs are working in some companies which are again a sub-set of the corporate sector. The real issue is 'character of corporate sector' and 'socio-economic value creation'. Unless the corporate sector is transformed, the MBAs will not be able to implement or practice ethical / moral values due to lack of context. Whole corporate sector should sincerely accept that 'profit & loss' is not the result of 'mechanics' of business—in the ultimate analysis it is the effort / creativity of human beings working for the companies. 'Mechanics of business' is guided by human beings not by computers or robots—otherwise MBAs would not have been required.

Human angle is very much involved in value/surplus creation. There is no inherent contradiction between profit and ethics except in the mindset of the so-called experts who are trying to confuse people by their interpretations due to their own predilection. A person requires food to maintain and develop his or her health. To maintain good health should be the focus not eating food. Smilarly the focus of the organisation should be creation of socio-economic value not profit maximisation. For maintaining health you can't take any food as you like or not bother about lifestyle. Similarly, for making profit you can't do whatever you like without bothering about society. The whole premise has to change. Focus should not be on profit or making money. B-schools should sincerely try to contribute to transform the mindset of the MBAs as well as the corporate sector.

It is also a fact that many CEOs / top business leaders has been found involved in corruption and manipulation to further their /family's interest or their masters' interest at the cost of ethics /corporation's interest or society's interest.

B-schools should start revisiting and redesigning their whole education-cultural environment if they really bother to contribute to the society. There is no point in creating a few so-called elite who will get special treatment and privileges but their social contribution would be very negligible. Socio-economic value creators are required not the so-called managers who are too busy to manage their own career graph at the cost of everything else.

'Manage / Managers'–these words are themselves having negative attitude or connotation which is manipulative in nature. This does not motivate to be concerned for the society or the country. The time has come to transform the managers to 'socio-economic value creators'. The name itself will drive positively to motivate and inspire individual. India's leading business schools are yet to wake up to this crucial aspect of management education.

The character of the B-schools is required to be changed.It is high time that they also should start introspecting and think how to transform their minds. A tentative guideline is suggested:

- Functional knowledge is necessary but not sufficient.
- Produce socio-economic value creators not balancesheet managers.
- Ethics should be integral part of the learning process and cultural environment of B-school.
- Institute should be the partner of the society and not the isolated 'elitist entity'.
- Institute should connect with corporate community as well as civic society and contribute in bringing efficiency in managing the corporation, civic society in terms of better ideas, innovations, developmental issues, mangerial practices, social practices etc. and

to provide leadership to change the cultural context for value creation which will benefit the maximum number of citizens.

- Students should be clearly told that society and business are much more complex and dynamic which cannot be taught in the clsssroom. They should not carry any false sense of an elitist ego. They should remember that half the world's most successful entrepreneurs are not even graduates,let alone post-graduates.
- A B-school should genuinely become the mentor & guide for unleashing the potential of thousands of talented people in civic/corporate community to bring revolutionary changes in the whole concept of value creation.
- Evolve parameters to evaluate the contribution towards socio-economic value creation.

It is absolutely imperative that management institutes that groom the nation's future pool of corporate managers have the very highest pedigree interms of curricula,faculty and academia-industry interface. Both the health of the corporate outfits, as well as the qualitative advancement of their manpower, hinges on how effectively and quickly B-schools adopt to the changing requirements as much of the students as of the corporate recuiters. Also germane to any business management education process is the constant fostering of the right moral values and human principles even as students are taught how to pursue a clearcut career.

MBA is not the panacea for all that bedevils the business organisations. Some of the most famous business leaders in India/world never went to a management institute. Genuine leaders would require an innate sense of right or wrong and a sense of socio-economic values or insights. Mark H. McCormack's comment is very relevant : "Business demands innovations. There is a constant need to feel around the fringes, to test the edges, but business schools, out of necessity, are condemned to teach the past. This not only perpetuates conventional thinking; it stifles innovation. I once heard someone say that if Thomas Edison had gone to business school we would all be reading by larger candles."

A B-school should develop appropriate contexts to develop socio-economic value creators instead of the so-called executives. For value creation, creativity / innovativeness is required to be practised. Time has come to re-name the B-school / Management Institute as 'Institute of socio-economic value creation" or 'Learning centre for socio-economic value creation' which should create context in which the desired intellectual, physical, social and moral attributes can be developed and facilitated. B-school should try to follow what Einstein said: "I never teach my pupils, I only attempt to provide the conditions (context) in which they can learn."

B-school should initiate dialogue and consultation between B-school and private / public organisations to continuously enrich management education and keep it updated to improve socio-economic value creation activities and inspire the students, corporate community and society at large in this direction. B-school should remember : "to teach others one must have a badge of authority; otherwise teaching becomes a mockery," So said Sri Ramakrishna Paramahansa.

Value Creation : Ceo and Board

In simple terms value means the capacity to satisfy human needs and demands. Value which is created with socio-economic insights or keeping in view the socio-economic-environmental issues is considered socio-economic value.

Value is created by mind-work. Main factors of value creation: technology, information/knowledge, creativity and implementation or actions, and all these factors are also products of mind-work. The process of value creation is the application and integration of these factors. All these factors are quite complex, dynamic and always in the process of change or flux. Knowledge is nobody's monopoly. No one is the controller or distributor of information / knowledge or creativity.

How to use / apply and integrate is the most critical issue the organisation has to address. The knowledge of 'how to use /integrate' is the key driving force and differentiator. This knowledge ultimately is the outcome of collective knowledge /wisdom or collective mind-work.

Sustained value creation should not be left to one individual or CEO. This is beyond the brilliance of one individual or two individuals. At the most CEO can play the role of 'Chief Encouragement Officer' or facilitator to create context for value creation.

Organisations should accept and appreciate 'distributive leadership' as the most critical factor for socio-economic value creation. CEOs should sincerely accept : "We must learn our limits. We are all something, but none of us everything" as stated by Blaise Pascal.

Core people of the organisation often think they know it all. Distributive or collective leadership is rare. Very few on the top really have the sincerity to listen to others. They believe their experience is the only valid one and the experience and opinions of others are invalid. Real knowledge grows only when it recognises the validity of all human experiences and does not discount the experiences and opinion of others. Unfortunately, organisational context does not often encourage openness. Sometimes, the boss is so insecure that any candid feedback may endanger the future of the feedback giver. Rosabeth Moss Kanter, Professor,

Harvard Business School commented in a recent interview: "A lot of scandals are because of CEOs who are arrogant. And then, when things slip, they bring power back into a closed inner circle and start cutting other people out of the conversation. That makes the situation worse for the company."

CEOs often suffer from the problem of information overload without commensurate abilities to convert information into knowledge. Also most CEOs become lonely men. Most CEOs neither have time,nor the courage to seek feedback on their performance. Though some companies are having some kind of appraisal system, but very few CEOs have the time or inclination to analyse it and accept the feedback sincerely.

CEO should facilitate confidence-building in the 'context' or corporate character. Only contextual confidence can ensure open dialogue, debate, communication, consultation and more responsibility / accountability and ownership of the problems which motivate people to accept problems and try to solve the problems.

Hard reality has already clearly proved that rules, regulations and laws have failed to ensure socio-economic value creation and ethical practices by the corporations. Corporate governance will remain a mere jargon-only for preaching not for practice-unless the 'character' of the board is transformed. Character of the board is the real issue-rules and laws will play superficial role unless this basic issue is addressed sincerely.

Performance cards of several corporate boards are dismal &pathetic. They have miserably failed to guide the organisations on the right path and ensure integrity, morality and good conduct. Several books were written / re-written on 'corporate governance'. Several committees were formed, several audit methods / procedures were introduced, several codes of conduct were formulated—but nothing has changed on the ground. The Enron board failed to safeguard its shareholders' interests and contributed to the collapse of the seventh largest public company in the US. Their affiliated consulting powerhouse, Anderson, disappeared within months of the Enron collapse. In India, the over-enthusiastic board of Global Trust Bank was pushing for rapid growth through insider trading in the stock markets which finally led to the collapse of the bank.

We should bear in mind a fundamental fact—the mere existence of a law on the statute books does not prevent the occurrence of fraud, misconduct, crime, manipulation or ensure adherence to its provisions.

Basic reasons for the failure of the Board are:

- Lack of integrity
- Maximisation of personal interest
- Lack of competence
- Lack of trust
- Loop holes in accounting practices

The 'Board of Directors' is having the image of an elitist bureaucratic privileged class whose main objective is to manipulate the command and control structure of the organisation to maximise the interests of a few select group of people. The Board has become a 'self-serving group'.

The Board should understand the proper intersection of money and integrity. It should sincerely start realising that there is no inherent conflict between profitability and integrity. Transformation of 'character' is the most relevant issue, not the so-called corporate governance code. We should enlighten ourselves by the teaching of Sri Ramakrishna Paramahansa: "He is truly a man to whom money is only a servant; but on the other hand, those who do not know how to make a proper use of it, hardly deserve to be called men."

The 'Board of Directors' should be redefined and renamed as the 'Committee of Collective Conscience and Wisdom' to facilitate and guide socio-economic value creation and accordingly control internal structure and governance of the organisation.

'Institution' cannot be built unless the character of the Board is transformed. The challenge of transformation of character is really tough since a paradigm shift, from promoters' / shareholders' interest to the 'social interest' is required to be achieved. Balancesheet mentality is required to be replaced by socio-economic value creation mentality.

But there is no alternative for the corporate sector. As Arun Maira correctly advised : "In recent times, the power of corporation has increased vis-à-vis other organs of society, including governments. There is danger in this if business corporations see their responsibility only towards their shareholders, and not more broadly towards society. Therefore the Board, the prime organ for corporate governance, must be held responsible for the broader role and responsibility of the corporation to society."

Bibliography

Desire, anger and greed—this triple gate of hell brings about the ruination of the soul. Therefore, one should avoid all these three.-

Bhagavad Gita

Hypocrisy, arrogance and pride—and anger, sternness and ignorance too—these are the marks of him, who is born with demoniac properties.-

Bhagavad Gita

A list major books which have been consulted or referred during the writing of this book is given. However, this list is not exhaustive.

1. Marketing Management, The Millennium Edition, Philip Kotler Prentice-Hall of India Pvt. Ltd, 2000.
2. The Mind Of The Strategist, Kenichi Ohmae, Penguine Books, 1982.
3. In Search Of Excellence, Tom Peters and Bob Waterman, Warner Books, 1988.
4. Managing Radical Change-What Indian companies must do to become world Class, Sumantra Ghoshal, Gita Piralmol and Christopher A. Bartlett, Viking, 2000.

5. The Bhagavad Gita or The Song Of Divine, Gita Press, Gorakhpur, India, Fiftyfith Reprint, 2004.
6. The Seven Habits Of Highly Effective people, Steven R.Covey, Simon & Schuster.
7. What They Don't Teach you at Harvard Business School, Mark H. McCormack, Fontana / Collins,1986.
8. Kautilya The Arthashastra, L.N. Rangarajan, Penguine Books, 1992.
9. Kautilay's Arthashastra-its Contemporary Relevance, IMCER & TF, 2005.
10. The Third Wave, Alvin Toffler, Bantam Books, 1980.
11. Future Shock, Alvin Toffler, Bantom Books, 1980.
12. Power shift, Alvin Toffler, Bantom Books, 1991.
13. The Welch Way-24 Lessons From The world's Greatest CEO, Jefferey A. Krames, Tata Mc Graw-Hill, 2003.
14. Thoughts to Inspire & Celebrate Ramkrisna, Gajanan Khergamker, Jaico, 2003.
15. The Prophet of Modern India-A Biography of Swami Vivekananda, Gautam Ghosh, Rupa & Co, 2003.
16. The Future At The Bottom Of The Pyramid, C. K. prahalad, Wharton School of publications, 2005.
17. The Circle Of Innovation, Tom Peter, Vintage Books, 1999.
18. People and Performance, Peter Drucker, Butterworth-Heinemann, 2004.
19. The New Realities, Peter Drucker, ButterWorth-Heinemann, 2004.
20. Winning, Jack Welch, Harper Collins, 2005.

21. You Can Win, Shiv Khera, Macmillan, Revised edition, 2004.

22. Count Your Chickens Before They Hatch, Arindam Chaudhari, Vikas, 2005.

23. Ten Deadly Marketing Sins: Signs and Solutions, Philip Kotler, John Wiley & Sons, Inc, 2004.

24. Ignited Minds, A P J Abdul Kalam, Penguin Books, 2003.

25. The Message of The Gita, edited by Anilbaran Roy, Sri Aurobindo Ashram Pondicherry, 1999.

26. The Ten Demandments : Rules to live in the age of Demanding Customer, Tata McGraw-Hill, 2004.

27. The Future Of Competition, C.K.Prahalad / Venkat Ramaswamy, Penguin Books India, 2004.

Reference/ Notes-

Several articles, write-ups, topics and reports were consulted, referred from various magazines, journals, newspapers. It is not possible to individually mention the name of the specific atricles / topics since hundreds of articles, reports, write-ups from various issues have been consulted or referred. Only name of the magazines, nespapers or journals except Harvard Business Review are listed below:

1. Business World
2. Indian Management, The Journal Of the All India Management Association
3. Business India
4. India Today
5. Business Today
6. Pitch

7. The Telegraph, Newspaper
8. The Times Of India, Newspaper
9. The Economic Times, Business newspaper
10. The Indian express, Newspaper
11. Annual Reports of Three companies including two fortune 500 company

Articles from Harvard Business Review

12. What Leaders Really Do, John P. Kotter, May-June 1990.
13. Manager and Leaders : Are They Different, March-April, 1992.
14. Leading Change : Why Transformation Efforts fail, John P. Kotter, March-April, 1995.
15. Musings on Management, Henry Mintzberg, July-august 1996.
16. What is Strategy, Michael E.Porter, November-December 1996.
17. Strtegic Renewal for Business Units, John O. Whitney, July-August 1996.
18. Building Your Company's Vision, James C. Collins and Jerry Porras, September-October 1996.
19. Competing For The Future, Gary Hamel and C.K. Prahalad, July-August 1994.
20. The Core Competence of the Corporation, C.K. Prahalad and Gary Hamel, May-June 1990.

Index